THE ADVENTURES OF A YORKSHIRE PHILOSOPHER

DAVID MIDGLEY

WOODBRIDGE
PUBLISHERS

Forest House, 3rd Floor 16-20
Clements Road Unit #2048
Ilford, IG1 1BA

ISBN (Paperback): 978-1-917526-41-8

ISBN (Hardback): 978-1-917526-42-5

Cover Design by Woodbridge Publishers.

ACKNOWLEDGEMENTS

There are many people to thank. Firstly David Blamires, who started this by asking for 500 words for the Parish magazine, which led to the first 2500 words.

To Scott Roberts and Mike Waring for taking the time to read the first drafts and encouraging me to continue.

To the CLB, the companies I have worked for, School of Philosophy and all the people who have shared my adventures.

Last but not least, my wife, for putting up with me talking about it for the last three years.

CONTENTS

CHAPTER ONE

ADVENTURES IN THE FAMILY AND THE CHURCH LADS BRIGADE

I was born in Bradford, West Yorkshire, to a mother from Halifax who had once worked as an usherette and a father from Bradford who had been employed in the mills.

We lived in a council house on an estate in the hills surrounding Bradford, later made famous by the film *Rita, Sue and Bob Too,* which was set in the same area and at the same time. I first watched the film in Edinburgh a few years later. I had avoided it initially because, like the sitcom *The Royle Family,* I thought it was a documentary.

I don't have many recollections of my early childhood, though I do remember the cat using my box of toy soldiers as a litter tray and my sister biting the heads off those soldiers. She later married one—a real soldier, that is. Let's stop there, shall we? So, I'll start with the events I can just about remember.

In the early years, there were six of us at home: my Mum, Dad, four sisters, an elder brother, and me. I was the second youngest. At that time, my father was not working because he only had one lung, and Mum had her hands full looking after us. Breakfast was on the table before we went to school. My mum kept a very clean house. We had a greenhouse made out of plastic sheeting and a well-kept vegetable patch. Looking back, we had no money, but we didn't know it. We were well looked after; up until the age of 15, we had to be in bed by 9 p.m. My father kept a bar of green carbolic soap hanging over the top shelf in the kitchen to remind us that if we swore, we'd get our mouths washed out with it.

We had a one-day holiday every year at Whitsun, when we went to see my grandma in Ravenscliffe, on the other side of Bradford. On that day, we wore our best clothes and met with our cousins from Homewood for a day of games and a buffet tea. Besides that and school trips, we never left the estate except to go to the woods in the nearby village of Shelf.

I remember Bonfire Night being a big deal. A few families from our street got together to celebrate Guy Fawkes' attempt to blow up the government centuries ago. There were the Crossleys, the Farrels, the Averys, and others. Each family provided something for the communal feast: toffee apples, Parkin, and bonfire toffee that could break your teeth. My family always seemed to contribute the pork pies and mushy peas.

We, the kids, would spend the six weeks leading up to Bonfire Night "chumping" for wood—gathering it from woodlands, people's gardens, or other streets' wood stocks (also known as raiding). Any old furniture or mattresses would go onto the fire. Building it was a work of art. Finding the centre pole was like winning the pools.

There were always fireworks. Every street had its own bonfire, and on the night itself, and for the next few days, the smell of smoke hung in the air. Since it was November, it was often wet and cold, making it difficult to get the fire going. Nothing that a couple of pints of petrol couldn't sort out.

In our family, coming of age was at 15. This was because my older sisters were at the age when you would leave school at 15 to start work. I remember one of my older sisters having a party at the house with friends and family present, and I'm sure that all my elder sisters had similar celebrations. The centrepiece was always a birthday cake.

Overall, it was a good childhood.

I remember one winter night when it was dark and cold. I was standing next to my brother Ian in St. Aidan's church hall around 7 o'clock. I was nearly 10, and Ian was nearly 15. It must have been a Monday because that was when the Young Boys Club (YBC) met, followed by the Junior Training Corps (JTC).

The Church Lads Brigade was the youth organisation of the Church of England. Why not the Scouts? There weren't any. The area was a bit rough for Scouts. The CLB has quite a history, with Church Lads' battalions fighting as units in WWI.

There were three levels: YBC (Young Boys Club) for ages 7-9, JTC (Junior Training Corps) for ages 10-15, and SC (Senior Corps) for ages 15-21. All were under the watchful eye of Mr. Robertshaw, the commanding officer. It had Privates, Lance Corporals, Sergeants, and officers and was run on a military footing—just without the guns.

The JTC was run by Mrs. Dennison, who was Mr. Robertshaw's sister.

In later years, as an adult, I would hear people talk about Roger and Silvia, casually referring to them by their first names. But for me, even after all those years, I could only think of them as Mr. Rob and Mrs. D—the nicknames we gave them as children.

I was put into the JTC because I was nearly 10, and my brother was asked to return because he was just old enough to join the Senior Corps (SC), which met on Fridays. How did we get there? I don't really know. It was around 1971. The four-year age difference between my brother and me meant we didn't spend much time together. So why did we end up at St. Aidan's Church Hall that night? Our family wasn't religious, so it was probably because I was just bored. These were the days when, if you came home during the six-week summer holidays, your mother would immediately send you back out again with a "Go play with the tyres on the bus." Obviously, there was no internet, no electronic games, and daytime TV was in its infancy.

I can only guess that either my mum or dad sent us there to get us out of the house.

I remember little from that first night. Strangely, Andy Rad and Steve Bentley must have been there, but I can't recall them. What I do remember is a middle-aged woman with a big bosom, dark brown curly hair, and glasses—Mrs. D, I think she wore a uniform. Her assistant was her beige-trousered, moss-green-jumpered, pipe-smoking, balding husband, who looked on quietly. With my memory now so hazy, how can I recall what he wore? Because he wore the same clothes for the next 20 years. Mr. and Mrs. Dennison were to become important figures in my life.

I met up with Mrs. D recently after many years; unfortunately, Mr. D had passed away. She remembered me well and remarked that I was always angry or on the verge of being angry. I don't recognise that version of myself, but others have said the same.

Marching, football, games, and making things come to mind as typical activities on a JTC night.

"Form up, dress to the right, attention, stand easy, by the left, quick march. Left, right." Every third Sunday was the Church Parade. For the first few times, we just marched behind the SC (Senior Corps) band—big bass drum, cymbals, side drums, and bugles. If you were posh, there was even a glockenspiel. Then came the JTC, with some in full uniforms, some with just a cap and belt, and then newcomers like me who had nothing. After a few weeks of attendance, you earned a cap and belt, and eventually, maybe six months later, you got the full uniform.

The band would march through the council estate, attempting to encourage the locals to attend church. I'm sure the drums and bugles playing loudly on a Sunday morning outside their front doors inspired many to come. However, the church was never full. In church, the CLB lads always sat in the back rows. Our aim was to sing louder than the choir, which we did—though perhaps not quite as well. During the service, when the collection plate was passed around, I put in the 2p coin given to me by my mum.

My mum particularly enjoyed the Church Lads' Mother's Day parade, where we were given small bouquets of flowers to take home. Since Ian and I were both in the CLB, she got two. I think that's all she got for Mother's Day. On Palm Sunday, we were given a cross made from a palm leaf.

It wasn't long before a group of us from the rough side of the estate had enlisted. Those who lived above the church always seemed a bit better off, residing in private homes, and most of their parents attended church. On the other side of the church was the council estate where David Crossley, the Cromptons, the Ridealishes, Andy Rad, Steve, a few others, and I lived. Having a few of us living close to each other was very useful when walking home at 9 p.m. on the estate, especially when we were wearing our uniforms.

Even without uniforms, you could find yourself in the wrong place at the wrong time. One night, Steve and I were followed by a group of lads intent on causing trouble, so we quickly made our way to Andy's house. Andy, who needed to shave at 14 years old and was six feet tall, joined us. All three of us then walked straight towards the gang following us, and they decided they needed to be somewhere else.

I do remember being threatened with a knife one night and, on another occasion, being hit on the head by a rock on the Boulevard (a street of flats opposite the entrance to the church). But this was normal estate life, where most gangs were based on the street you lived on. If you were walking on the wrong street, you were asking for trouble. On one particular night in October, a group of us were walking in a nearby street when a young lad, no older than five, stood alone at his garden gate and shouted, "They've come to nick our wood!" Before we knew it, lads appeared from everywhere, ready to defend their bonfire wood. We made a quick exit to more familiar streets.

Why did I stay in the Church Lads? I don't know—perhaps it was better than watching *Coronation Street.* "Do not talk during *Coronation Street.* If you want to talk, go out."

"But Mum, it's snowing."

"I don't care; now be quiet while I watch this."

They say you pick up things from your parents. Well, I've always hated soaps.

My first camp was at Apperley Bridge, on the other side of Bradford. I was around twelve. Ian and I didn't have sleeping bags (what were they?). My mum stitched together some flannelette sheets to make into bags, and we took our pyjamas. No one at camp wore pyjamas. Ian and I never wore them again.

It was a battalion camp with people from Queensbury, Bierley, and Buttershaw. Some of us from Buttershaw got collared by officers from Queenie and ended up peeling potatoes in the canteen. I had never peeled potatoes before—my mum did that—and it wasn't long before my fingers were cut to ribbons. The officers told us to go away as the potatoes were covered in blood. That night, we were freezing, sleeping in tents for the first time. None of our officers were present, and we seemed to be getting more than our fair share of crappy jobs. The next morning, a few of us got on the bus and went home.

There's a photograph of some of the JTC in uniform around a display of musical instruments. This was about 48 years ago, and I'm still in contact with many of them.

I looked so forlorn. Yes, I'm the one standing on the far right. Years later, Andy, who became an artist, painted my portrait from this photo for my 50th birthday. It hangs on my wall at home.

Years passed, and things at home weren't going well. My mother suffered three strokes, which left one side of her body paralysed. She was unable to walk upstairs and was confined to a bed in the living room. We watched TV while she sat on a steel bucket to go to the toilet. My elder sisters left to live with various boyfriends, and my dad ran off with a woman called Vera, who lived across the road. This left just my younger sister Gwen, my brother Ian—who had left the CLB when he started work at 16—and me.

The house deteriorated quickly as there was only myself at thirteen, my sister at eleven, and our invalid mother. I remember the cat licking the fat from the chip pan because no one was feeding it and the smell of cat poo in the living room because there was no one to clean it up. The vegetable patch and greenhouse disappeared, and the garden became overgrown. We went from having little money to practically no money. The council provided home help for a few days a week.

I slept on a mattress on the floor in my bedroom, which had no carpet. I thought it was cool, but the reality was I had no bed or carpet.

When I reached 15, it was my turn to come of age. Things are different now. I didn't expect a party or a fuss, and I wasn't bothered. Leaving school was now at 16, and the family seemed to have scattered with marriages, births, and deaths. Even though we were even poorer by then, my mother insisted on getting me a birthday cake. I never liked sponges, so the local bakery produced a fruit cake in the shape of a football. It was covered in white icing with round discs of chocolate, each bearing the name of a legendary Leeds player from the 70s. It was expensive—around £60. My mother couldn't afford it, but I think, for her, it was a duty; whatever the older children received, I would receive—a remembrance of happier times. There was no party.

The CLB was always there.

Camps improved over time. I can't remember them all, but a few stand out.

There was the weekend at Malham, where Steve ate seven peanuts and proceeded to fart seven times—so loudly that even I, in a separate tent, could hear him and the groans of those sleeping in the same tent.

Then, there was Cullingworth, where we had to build snow walls around the tents to reduce the wind chill. Two tents were joined with tarpaulin, with a heater placed in between, as the surrounding area was cut off due to four-foot-deep snow. On Sunday morning, when we broke camp, the places where we had slept had formed coffin shapes in the snow. This was a time before risk assessments.

Kettlewell was memorable for our stay at the youth hostel perched at the top of the hill. It was freezing cold, and when I split my jeans from my groin to my knee, I had to wrap a Leeds scarf around my leg to preserve my dignity.

By this time, I was in the Senior Corps, and over a few months, the group had built a canoe from scratch. We decided to canoe from Keighley to Skipton. We had two canoes—one that we had built ourselves and another that had been bought second-hand. I initially got into the canoe we had built, sitting behind Dave Blamires, a senior member of the group. However, it felt so unsafe that I immediately said, "No thanks," and got out, much to the scorn of the group. The bottom of the canoe was loaded with tins of beans, soup, and Smash to save the weight for those walking on foot. After I was criticised for being "daft and soft," someone else took my place. As soon as David pushed off from the towpath, the canoe capsized. The guys in the canoe were soaked, of course—no life jackets—and were scrambling to get out of the canal as quickly as possible. Mr D, ever the practical one, asked them to get back into the canal to retrieve the tins, saying, "You're already wet." He was told where to go. To my knowledge, the tins are still there.

Eventually, we set off again, and I remember canoeing through Skipton with Nick Kenny, the ducks making noises that sounded suspiciously like laughter. We camped in a local park, where we soon encountered a group of local youths curious about what was going on.

Things started to get a bit leery until one of the older guys with us locked his back, and we had to ask the lads where the nearest phone was to call an ambulance. We did, and when the ambulance arrived and took the guy to the hospital, the locals lost interest, and everyone went to bed.

It was on this trip, at Silsden under a bridge over the canal, that I misjudged the amount of water needed for the mashed potato, ending up with potato soup instead—much to the consternation of the other guys. I wasn't asked to cook again, so I consider that a win.

St Aidan's had a marching band made up of a side drum, bass drum, and bugle, with a flag in the middle. I played the bugle, though I confess I wasn't very good. There was once a competition for the best bugle player in the battalion. We had to play the "Last Post" in a hall where the judges were hidden behind a screen to prevent bias. Halfway through, I forgot the tune and ended up playing for about five minutes, repeating the bits I knew in a desperate attempt to remember the ending. I never did, and eventually, I just stopped playing, paused in the now deafening silence of the hall, turned around, and left.

We entered nationwide competitions with bands from other youth organisations, but we nearly always came last or close to it. On one occasion, we were commended on having a two-tone bass drum that Steve played. It was news to us that we even had a two-tone bass drum.

We always had our annual company camp during the spring bank holiday week. For some reason, and seemingly every camp, Steve, Andy, David Ford, and I were always given the task of digging the toilets—a job fitting our "lower end of the estate" status—hence the birth of the song "The Shit Digger Blues." The night before going on a week-long camp, I always made myself a large meal—eggs, chips, and beans with three slices of bread. I knew I'd have moments of hunger due to the variability of camp food, which ranged from bad to inedible.

A weekly camp near Hellifield stays in my mind for many reasons. I had always thought of myself as quiet, sullen, and unnoticed by others (a notion that has been confirmed by others quite recently)—not exactly ideal leadership material. However, at this camp, I was made a section leader, and to my surprise, I found that I liked it.

It didn't start well. Young Robert, Mr and Mrs D's youngest son, always had a lot to say, and he was getting on my nerves. In a moment of frustration, I threw an axe at him. Thankfully, he jumped out of the way—otherwise, who knows? However, I'd probably be out of prison by now. After that incident, we became friends and still are, even after a forty-year gap.

The section gelled well. Once I began talking to people in a friendly manner and treating them with respect, they responded in kind, and we ended up winning the camp award. I noticed a girl for the first time and fell in love. She was smart, pretty, and, most importantly, seemed happy to talk to me. The very innocent relationship lasted only a few weeks (I had no idea what to do... still don't), but the memory has stayed with me. Recently, I told the same girl, now a good-looking woman, that she was my first love—resulting in major embarrassment all around. It was a great week.

A few years later, we returned to the same campsite, but with different results as I was older and now frequenting hostelries. It was the last camp I attended. Steve and I decided to skip the camp dinner and went to the pub instead.

We had a few pints and dinner in the village of Hellifield, but at 10:30 p.m., the pub closed. Across the road from the pub was the WMC (Working Men's Club). We didn't think we'd be able to get in, not being members, but as we approached the door, the doorman asked if we were the new vicar's sons. We promptly answered, "Yes!"

We were in.

There was a disco on, and being drunk, we began dancing to the Skids' song *Into the Valley.* Soon, we were joined by some women. Great, this was going well—until I noticed some rather angry farmers giving us the dead eye as we danced with their girlfriends. I quickly pulled Steve out before we got ourselves killed. He had no idea what was going on. Mrs D gave us a good telling-off when we staggered back to our tent.

These were company camps, but there were also battalion camps.

The last battalion camp I remember attending was when I was sixteen, in Prestatyn, Wales. It was fantastic—I went out with three girls in one week, played a great game of football against the Boys' Brigade (though I did injure their best player in a rash tackle, heh heh), and became a hero to all the lads on site.

Somewhere along the way, and I don't know when or why, I started my own tradition at camp—a tradition I have never talked about until now. On the first night of any camp, I would go out alone at night, walking a distance away until I could no longer hear the noise of the camp. If I could, I'd find a spot in the woods or on a hill. There, I would undo my jacket and shirt and just let the cold breeze flow through and around my body as if it were cleansing the debris of the estate off me. It felt as though I was touching something beyond myself. I would now call it consciousness, but at the time, it just felt clean, clear, and still.

I still remember that feeling. I still long for that feeling. Here begins my journey into philosophy.

As I began working, I soon found myself on a permanent evening shift. This meant I could only make it to the Friday night meet just in time for football. By then, Steve, Andy, and the others had already moved on. I was being drawn away by the lure of alcohol, music, and girls, and I eventually left the Church Lads Brigade at around 19, after a decade behind the flag.

Steve, Andy, and I stayed in contact—Steve was my best man at my second wedding, and I was best man at both of his. We remain the best of friends. Andy now lives in Rome as a struggling artist, seemingly intent on dying in poverty and being "discovered" years after his death as an artistic genius. His sculptures are wonderful.

Many years later, more of the original CLB crew started to reconnect with me bit by bit through Facebook. Then I got some tickets for an Aussie Pink Floyd concert. At short notice, Steve couldn't make it, and another friend was on holiday. I remembered that Nick and Dave were Floyd fans and invited them to the concert with just a few days' notice. They both came, and we met after a 40-year hiatus. It was amazing—40 years felt like 40 minutes. We then began having regular meet-ups with some of the others. It has been a real delight. One night, Mr Robertshaw came along. I was in shock. It was wonderful to see him again.

So, what does the CLB mean to me? It's the foundation of all I have done. Even back then, I started looking for something beyond the physical. I was confirmed at 14 (like being baptised as an adult at Bradford Cathedral). But that wasn't enough. I don't know what it was supposed to satisfy, but it didn't.

Mrs D once said to me that I would spend my life looking for something. I think she was right. Recently, she told me she had no recollection of saying that to me, but for me, it was a seminal moment.

CHAPTER TWO

ADVENTURES IN POLITICS

I've always had an interest in politics, but it was around the age of 15 or 16 that my curiosity really deepened.

> "THE HISTORY OF ALL HITHERTO EXISTING SOCIETY IS THE HISTORY OF CLASS STRUGGLE.
>
> KARL MARX (1818–1883)"

Is it?

Most of society, I think, is based on greed.

Why was I interested in politics? I'm not entirely sure. Perhaps it was because I was poor and living on a rundown council estate. Maybe I really was angry, as everyone seemed to suggest. My mother and father both supported Labour, but I'm not certain they always voted. Politics wasn't a common topic of discussion in our family.

However, by the age of 15, I had joined the Young Socialists and the Workers Revolutionary Party. I attended rallies and meetings at a pub behind St Luke's Hospital in Bradford, where we planned to take over local radio stations.

(I was still in the CLB at this time—maybe I just wanted to belong? Hmm, I'll need to think about that.)

I once tried to read the *Communist Manifesto*, but I fell asleep—it was boring. And after reading a bit of Russian history, I wasn't keen on the idea of killing millions of people for a political theory that doesn't work and is really just another means of control.

Maybe I'm a socialist?

> “
>
> A POLITICAL AND ECONOMIC THEORY OF SOCIAL ORGANISATION WHICH ADVOCATES THAT THE MEANS OF PRODUCTION, DISTRIBUTION, AND EXCHANGE SHOULD BE OWNED OR REGULATED BY THE COMMUNITY AS A WHOLE.
>
> GOOGLE OXFORD LANGUAGES DEFINITION
>
> ”

That's closer to how I think about things, but it's still not quite there.

I had *News Line* (a socialist newspaper) delivered to our front door daily. No one in the family was bothered. The articles were a bit heavy going, but I was more interested in the constant battle to keep the paper going—the "fighting fund." These were the days when, after getting off the bus at Elland Road for the Leeds match, you either turned right to buy the *Bulldog* (the National Front paper) or turned left to buy *News Line* of the WRP.

The day I started work was the day I joined the union.

In my early days, politics was either centre-left (Wilson, Callaghan) or centre-right (Heath), but Maggie changed all that.

This was the time of the Winter of Discontent—unions continually on strike, British Leyland, the three-day week, Red Ken in London, and left-wing councils like Liverpool.

The unions had become too powerful, too left-wing. Marxists and anarchists stopped the Labour government from imposing controls on strikes. The government fell, and Margaret Thatcher came to power, quickly imposing the controls on the unions that Labour had been unable to enforce.

I spent the next year selling papers and knocking on doors, with very little effect, until Thatcher's second election win—then I quit.

At the time, I was annoyed and couldn't understand how people could vote for her. I thought people just didn't care about social injustice. Later years taught me that what people really wanted was not to think but to live in a kind of waking sleep.

Aaargh, that's cynical. Let me try to explain.

People want an easy life. I believe that people live in different states of consciousness:

- **Asleep:** Generally unconscious, dreaming, out of it—whether in bed, on the sofa, or wherever. There's nothing wrong with being asleep.

- **Waking Sleep:** Awake but not truly awake. Spending time thinking about the past, the future, daydreaming about success, or fearing failure. Your thoughts are anywhere but in the present. Ever driven somewhere and then realised you don't know how you got there?

- **Awake:** Living in the moment. Being aware of all the possibilities open to you that exist all the time, but are often missed—especially the opportunity to be happy.

I got most of this from the School of Philosophy, but it's a common theme in many philosophical traditions.

Throughout this story, I will quote the Sanatan Dharma as described in the book *Good Company* by Shri Shantananda Saraswati, a teacher from India. He summed up 10 principles on how to try and lead a good life. You could just as well look up the Sermon on the Mount by Jesus or, I imagine, extracts from the Quran.

(Except, in the Sermon on the Mount, when they talk about being "meek," I have never understood how the meek should be blessed—I don't think they should.)

PRINCIPLE SIX

"

THERE IS A NATURAL COURSE OF USE OF THE SENSES, AND THESE CAN BE REGULATED; THE RULES ARE PRESCRIBED IN EVERY TRADITION, AND FROM THESE, ONE HAS TO LEARN HOW TO USE ONE'S SENSES WITHIN THOSE LIMITATIONS. ONE DOES NOT CURB THE USE OF SENSES BUT REGULATES THEM. THE CURBING OF EXCESSIVE USE WILL THEN TAKE PLACE NATURALLY.

SHRI SHANTANANDA SARASWATI, GOOD COMPANY (1987), THE STUDY SOCIETY

"

***

We are never in just one state, but, except for sleep, we generally do not know which state we are in—an undisciplined mind wandering with no control. We need to **control our senses**.

Obviously, being awake is what we want, but how do we achieve it?

This, I think, will be a recurring point in this story. On this occasion, talking about politics in the late 70s, people were awakened out of their Waking Sleep by electricity blackouts—they couldn't watch *Corrie,* there was constant bad news on the TV when it was on, right-wing newspapers screaming bad news, and four-day weeks reducing their wages.

I remember my mother during the four-day week, crying in the candlelight at home during a blackout. She was disabled and scared.

Fear wakes you up.

Then, someone comes along—Maggie, with her trickle-down economics—and says, *I can fix it for you, so you can go back to waking sleep.* The general electorate says, *Yes, please,* and in she gets.

Social justice, inequality, and the growing gap between rich and poor disappear if you can't watch the TV and put the heating on.

***

Trickle-Down Economics

Ever since Reagan and Thatcher first tried them, trickle-down policies have exploded budget deficits and widened inequality. At best, they've temporarily increased consumer demand (the opposite of what's needed during the high inflation that Britain and much of the world are experiencing).

REAGAN'S TAX CUTS AND DEREGULATION AT THE START OF THE 1980S WERE NOT RESPONSIBLE FOR AMERICA'S RAPID GROWTH THROUGH THE LATE 1980S. HIS EXORBITANT SPENDING (MOSTLY ON NATIONAL DEFENCE) FUELLED A TEMPORARY BOOM THAT ENDED IN A FIERCE RECESSION.

ROBERT REICH,
THE GUARDIAN (2022)

***

But the strikes decreased, and the lights stayed on. So, she was probably what was needed at that time.

As philosophers, should we care? **Yes... and no.**

No, because we live in a world of general selfishness and "dog eat dog," and we don't want to fall into the trap of behaving like that. Also, listening to the news can get you seriously depressed if you feel there is nothing you can do about it.

Yes, because living in the present and being awake is the key to understanding ourselves and the world. This understanding enables us to see the faults in ourselves and in others. Using this knowledge, it is our duty to give service to others and try to make the world a better place.

> REALITY IS AN ILLUSION, ALBEIT A VERY PERSISTENT ONE
>
> ALBERT EINSTEIN, BRAINYQUOTE.COM

Ubuntu Philosophy

In Africa, there is a philosophy called **Ubuntu** (Zulu pronunciation: [ùɓúnt'ù]), a Nguni Bantu term meaning "humanity." It is sometimes translated as:

> - I AM BECAUSE WE ARE (ALSO I AM BECAUSE YOU ARE), OR
> - HUMANITY TOWARDS OTHERS (ZULU: UMUNTU NGUMUNTU NGABANTU).
>
> SOURCE: WIKIPEDIA

We are just a sample of a population—a sample of humanity. (I knew my Master Black Belt in Six Sigma would come in handy someday.) We live in this society. Society influences us, and we influence society.

If we reflect or ponder on our daily behaviour, what would we think? How does it affect others? Does it improve society?

"

HAVING CONSIDERATION AND GIVING PARDON, BEING TOLERANT OF ALL THE DIFFICULTIES, AWKWARDNESS, AND FAULTS OF OTHERS, SO THAT YOU PROVIDE THEM WITH SPACE. IN DUE COURSE, WHEN THEY SEE NO REACTION, THEY MAY LEARN SOMETHING BETTER THAT YOU HOLD DEAR TO YOURSELF.

SHRI SHANTANANDA SARASWATI, GOOD COMPANY (1987), THE STUDY SOCIETY

"

There is a definite need to regularly sit and meditate to refresh and control the senses. Some people think that meditation alone is the answer. I think if everyone did it, it probably would be the answer. However, not everyone does.

Does living in that higher plane of consciousness put food on the table? Knowing that this life is just an illusion, as Einstein said, does it ensure the streets are safe and that we have good education and healthcare?

Yes, it does—but only if you recognise that and use that knowledge to better yourself and society by being an example.

Here's another Einstein quote:

“

THE WORLD IS A DANGEROUS PLACE TO LIVE; NOT BECAUSE OF THE PEOPLE WHO ARE EVIL, BUT BECAUSE OF THE PEOPLE WHO DON'T DO ANYTHING ABOUT IT.

ALBERT EINSTEIN, BRAINYQUOTE.COM

”

Jesus said:

“

GIVE UNTO CAESAR WHAT IS OWED TO CAESAR.

”

Or something like that.

Buddhist monks burned themselves alive in protest of the Vietnam War. I'm not recommending you do that, but the point is, as philosophers, we are not separate from this world.

Keep your head in the highest consciousness, but keep your feet on the ground.

Being conscious or awake means you have a duty to put your knowledge into practice. But few are aware of what consciousness means.

Did I say this was easy? It's not.

This may sound pretentious, I know. You do have to be careful—being awake doesn't make you right and everyone else wrong.

It is, I think, overly optimistic to believe that your example of being a good, kind person will change the world. But it is all we have. The alternative is to accept the current status or do what we usually do: moan about it.

Certainly, trying to push my ideas of what is right or wrong onto people who are not interested is like trying to teach a pig how to dance. It's a waste of time, and it annoys the pig.

The American author and speaker John C. Maxwell wrote:

“

MOST PEOPLE WANT TO CHANGE THE WORLD TO IMPROVE THEIR LIVES, BUT THE WORLD THEY NEED TO CHANGE FIRST IS THE ONE INSIDE THEMSELVES.

”

Everyone has an opinion on what is wrong with the world, yet few will do the work to improve the first problem area: themselves.

So, what is the work we need to do? Back to the Sanatan Dharma.

PRINCIPLE EIGHT

> "ONE HAS TO ACQUIRE TRUE KNOWLEDGE."

So, what is true knowledge?

Any knowledge that involves hatred, separation, "I'm better than you," control, or "you must do this," in my opinion, is not true knowledge.

Reading the *Vedas* (an ancient Indian philosophical text) would be great, but you don't have to. There are Western philosophies like those of Plato, Socrates, Descartes, Nietzsche, and many others that you can study. I don't agree with everything I read, and you must be careful not to disappear up your own arse, but with an open mind, you can begin to understand the nature of yourself and others. Gather knowledge if it seems good, put the knowledge into practice, review the results, keep doing it if it feels right, and stop it if it doesn't. Learn through experience and adapt.

Any knowledge that makes you look inside at yourself, for me, is true knowledge because we are a microcosm of the world we live in. What applies to us applies to everyone.

So, what do you do with all that internal knowledge?

Give service.

“SERVICE IS LOVE IN ACTION.

KEN ESSIEN”

Service is external; it's about looking outwards and doing things for reasons other than yourself. Do it for love.

We live in this world, and we have a part to play in it. Whether you agree with my politics or anyone else's, take part. Listen, form your own views by being awake, and make a difference.

But first, make a difference to yourself. Don't give in to that Waking Sleep.

“I ALONE CANNOT CHANGE THE WORLD, BUT I CAN CAST A STONE ACROSS THE WATERS TO CREATE MANY RIPPLES.

MOTHER TERESA”

The world can be a dangerous place. Recognise it, but don't let it scare you. Sometimes, we find ourselves in the wrong place at the wrong time, and there's nothing we can do about it. The only thing we can control is ourselves. Is it wishful thinking to believe that if you set an example, others will follow? Yes, but do it anyway.

Back to Politics

Forget your prejudices, public opinion, and the media. Wake up and see the world for what it is, in all its glory and despair. **Be the example of what you want the world to be.**

> “YOU SHOULD ONLY TAKE WHAT YOU DESERVE AND CONSIDER EVERYONE ELSE EQUALLY DESERVING. SO, DO NOT TAKE ANYTHING EXTRA—ALL THAT YOU ACCUMULATE EXTRA IS THEFT. TO STEAL FROM THE UNIVERSE DEPRIVES OTHER PEOPLE. SO DO NOT KEEP ANYTHING MORE THAN WHAT CAN BE EQUALLY AVAILABLE TO EVERYONE ELSE.
>
> SHRI SHANTANANDA SARASWATI, GOOD COMPANY (1987), THE STUDY SOCIETY”

CHAPTER THREE

ADVENTURES IN SCHOOL

I didn't like school. In infant and middle school, I was always in the highest class, but I don't think I was very popular. Maybe I was angry? Thinking back on how often I bathed (we didn't have a shower), I probably smelled as well.

At junior school, the teachers approached my mum and dad, suggesting I apply for a scholarship at Bradford Grammar School. Apparently, my parents replied that if the comprehensive school was good enough for my brothers and sisters, it was good enough for me, so they said no.

A year later, when I was 13, my mum became seriously ill. It was probably the last significant decision they made for me.

I had a burst ulcer at the age of 12, just as I started at the comprehensive school. I vomited and passed three to four pints of blood over a three-day period. Every time I tried to walk, I fainted. My parents called the doctor out. He said I was fine. Then, my dad showed him the bucket of black blood, and the doctor ran to the local phone box to call an ambulance.

I spent three weeks in Bradford's Children's Hospital, getting pumped full of blood. The first time I got out of bed was to watch England get knocked out of the World Cup qualifiers by Poland on TV.

I missed about two months of school and lived off Farley's rusks and Ski yoghurt for six months. Teachers kindly came to the house to give me some home tuition, but when I went back to school, I always felt like I was catching up.

Photos taken of me at the comprehensive school showed a boy who, these days, might be voted in yearbooks as "Most Likely to Become a Serial Killer."

When I look back, I have a strong feeling that I wanted to belong, but I never quite did. Was it my poverty? (Three or four of us out of 30+ in the class had to walk to the front of the room every day to get our free school meals.) Did I smell? Was I just moody? I don't know. Although people thought I was bright, I don't think I fulfilled their expectations.

At home, there were no expectations. With the issues surrounding my mother's illness, other priorities took precedence—like getting something to eat and washing clothes.

At school, as the fifth of six Midgleys, I was just another estate kid. I was in an A form (the good old comprehensive system), the first in my family at that level. When the deputy head first read my name out in French class, he said, "Midgley! As in Mary, Ian, Susan, Lynn Midgley?"

"Yes, sir."

"What are you doing in an A form?"

"Don't know, sir."

It was, though, a rough school.

I've seen schools that proudly list their students who went to Oxford or Cambridge universities. We, on the other hand, had a list of those who ended up in Armley or Strangeways prisons (not true, but it felt that way).

The science teacher introduced us to his assistant, who we'd need to deal with if we didn't behave or complete our homework. The assistant was a rubber Bunsen burner pipe, which he slapped hard on the workbench.

In our first week, the history teacher walled up a boy who gave him some backchat.

I once had to write an essay on budgerigars as punishment for laughing in class when a boy had chewing gum thrown into his hair.

My mate Greg poured soup on another friend's head at dinner. The deputy head pulled him into his office and said the problem was that he lacked respect. He then punched Greg in the stomach.

I was once smacked on the bottom by my own pump in front of everyone on the football field for swearing at my fellow defender, who hadn't stopped an attack. **My own pump!**

On the last morning of school, we had our first O-level exam in the afternoon. The girls in the class were crying, and the boys were very quiet.

I remember telling myself, *Don't regret leaving; you've never liked school. Don't look back.* I never did. I left with four O-levels and three CSEs—not exactly setting the world alight.

I finished my last exam on a Tuesday and started work the following Monday at 16 and a half.

Friends for Life

> ALL THE WORLD'S A STAGE, AND ALL THE MEN AND WOMEN MERELY PLAYERS. THEY HAVE THEIR EXITS AND THEIR ENTRANCES; AND ONE MAN IN HIS TIME PLAYS MANY PARTS.
>
> AS YOU LIKE IT,
> WILLIAM SHAKESPEARE

I'm used to people entering my life, becoming important, and then exiting, it's part of working life. But there have been more permanent friendships.

I don't know if it's the same everywhere else, but in Yorkshire, people tend to be slow to make friends. Once established, though, you are friends for life.

I have people in my life who have been friends for most of my life.

At 15, I met the Frogs. Andy Rad's mother was Italian, and his father was Ukrainian. His sister, Lida, was born in Bradford but was married to a Frog, Chris. He had been her French teacher in school.

They lived near Paris and worked as English teachers. They came over in the summer and at Christmas to see Lida's and Andy's mum.

One day, I think it was Andy's birthday, they took Andy and me on a trip to Lincoln.

I had rarely been in a car before, never mind been to Lincoln (it took another 45 years before I went back). I was quiet. They brought a picnic, which we ate on the grounds of Tattershall Castle. There was some very strange food—round slices of spotty meat with a funny taste. I refused; it smelled and tasted wrong.

They offered me some wine. URGH.

Eventually, they offered me some chicken, and I started to eat. "It's a French chicken," said Chris. I stopped eating. *What will I catch?*

I mention these people because they were another major influence on me. They were sarcastic, political, and constantly arguing. Wow, could they argue—in Italian, French, and English?

But they were also generous, kind, and supportive. I think they were basically hippies.

They showed me another way of life when all I had known was the life of the council estate and the CLB.

One Christmas Eve, when I was around 18, we headed out to the pub. I walked up to Andy's, where Lida was running late getting ready. Chris had a 1.5-litre plastic bottle of cheap red wine, and between us, we drank it in 30 minutes. We then went to the pub, where I drank six pints of lager.

When I got home, I didn't have a bed—just a mattress on the floor, as I mentioned earlier. There was no carpet, just floorboards, and the walls were covered in lining paper that I had painted a coffee colour. (I kid you not; I have absolutely no taste.) The next morning, on Christmas Day, I woke to find the walls in my bedroom dripping with what looked like blood. It was, in fact, the red wine I had vomited the night before. **Happy days.**

Despite moments like that, I've been fortunate in maintaining long-lasting friendships. Besides the Frogs, who I still see, Andy Rad, Steve, and others from the CLB remain close friends to this day. The Frogs' children and husbands are now friends too. Over the years, they've been joined by other, more recent friends. I consider myself incredibly lucky to have such good friends I might not see for years, yet we can always pick up right where we left off.

Reflecting on my early years, I share these stories to provide context for what happened later. I'm not looking for sympathy or pity, I don't see myself as a victim of society. This was just the way things were. A few years ago, someone described me as one of those people who "pulled themselves up by their bootstraps." I don't quite recognise that description either. If anything, maybe I should have pulled those straps a bit tighter.

CHAPTER FOUR

ADVENTURES AT WORK

The Start of My Stellar Career

Not quite.

At school, I went to see the careers adviser and said I wanted to be a journalist. The adviser told me to think again and suggested looking toward the mill. At that time, textiles was the major industry in Bradford. I had a few interviews with local companies, mostly for office jobs, but I didn't get anywhere. There was no suggestion of going to university or 6th form, given the family circumstances.

My great-uncle worked at a textile mill in Buttershaw, a place known for recruiting people from the same family. They believed that peer pressure would keep everyone in line. My mum suggested I go down and ask for a job.

I went to the mill and asked for Neville Pearson, the day shift manager. I asked if there were any vacancies. He asked if I had any relatives at the company, and I mentioned my Uncle Thomas. He then asked what I was doing at school. I told him I was taking O-levels. Neville pulled out three coloured pens and asked me to identify the colours. I answered, "Red, black, and blue." He went into the next office to see the site manager, Mr. Wright. Within 60 seconds, he came back and said I could start on Monday as an apprentice overlooker. The entire interaction took about 10 minutes.

Later in my career, I had five interviews for the same job, with presentations and online exams, and still didn't get the position. How have times changed?

A week after my last exam, I joined Bulmer and Lumb, and that was that. At sixteen and a half, I began my working life.

Although I started as an apprentice, my first job was as a "bump presser." A bump was a compressed parcel of wool that came from a gilling machine. Each machine produced two containers of wool every 20 minutes, and there were six machines. My job was to compress the wool on a machine and tie it off to create a 20kg bump. These bumps were then sent down a short wooden slide for the next man, who put eight bumps into a bale, tied it off, and prepared it for transport to the customer.

In an eight-hour shift, I was expected to create 120 bumps. It was the lowest job in the mill. Since the company sold the wool by weight, moisture tests were done to ensure at least 20% water content. If the wool didn't meet that threshold, workers would pour water on the bales to increase their weight. I heard rumours of people urinating on the bales to get the weight up, but that's unconfirmed.

I was trained by a young lad named Danny. He couldn't have been older than 18, and I had seen him around the estate. Danny, unfortunately, had a short temper, and he was often in trouble with the law. Once, I was sitting with Danny and some other lads when his ex-girlfriend showed up to dispel a rumour he had started—that she had VD. He claimed he knew because, when he'd put his hand up her skirt, he'd felt something scabby.

Proudly, she told us that she'd been to the doctor and didn't have VD—she had herpes.

Though Danny was tough with others, he was great with me. He showed me how to operate the press as his backup in case he was off ill. Unfortunately for me, Danny left to visit relatives in Australia for three months, which meant I was stuck on the press for four months before I started any real apprenticing. The job was physically demanding, but I got fit and lost a lot of weight. Still, it was a tough transition from school to full-time work.

My first weekly wage was £27. Out of that, £15 went straight to my mother for board, leaving me with £12 for myself.

Happily, every lunchtime, the lads from the mill played football on some scrap land next to the main building. We used jumpers as goalposts. The teams were made up of mixed abilities and ages, and I loved the game. It was during these football matches that I earned the nickname "Legs." Apparently, the better footballers couldn't get past me because I would trip them up.

One of the overlookers (supervisors) was an older man named Walter, who had once played for Bradford Park Avenue. He was over 60, and though his touch was still fantastic, his legs were long gone. Once, during a match, I neatly pushed the ball past him on one side and ran around him on the other. I didn't make it far. Walter grabbed hold of my balls as I tried to pass him, and I ended up writhing on the floor in agony.

"You don't take the mick out of your elders," he said.

It was painful, but a good lesson learned.

Eventually, Danny came back, and I transitioned to my apprentice role in the pre-combing gilling department. My Overlooker was a man named Donald McDonald. Yes, really.

I didn't realise that being an apprentice wasn't just about learning the job—it was all-encompassing. It involved working, socialising, and even lessons in life. Donald took it upon himself to teach me everything a young man "needed to know," from women to drinking. He looked like Noel Edmunds, who was quite popular at the time. I, being slightly sarcastic (you don't believe me, do you?), constantly pushed his patience. Donald tried to beat the sarcasm out of me—sometimes literally. Once, Neville walked in on Donald, kicking me in the head next to a machine.

"Just training him, Donald?"

"Aye, he finds it hard to learn," Donald replied.

Neville just walked off. Donald broke my glasses five times in the first six months.

I also failed miserably at picking up the girl at the opticians, where I became a regular visitor due to my frequent broken glasses. This failure with women became a bit of a theme in my life.

Donald, on the other hand, fancied himself quite the ladies' man. He often took me around Bradford to pubs and nightclubs, trying to show me how to pick up women. I was terrible at it, and in retrospect, I think the women have more sense than we gave them credit for. The places Donald took me weren't exactly hotspots for young people—they were more for the middle-aged crowd. I was only seventeen, and the women there seemed to be looking for a drink, a chat, and perhaps a bit of harmless flirting before heading back home to their husbands and kids. The men seemed to be after the same thing, though sometimes they wanted more.

I remember one time Donald was trying to get rid of an old girlfriend in a pub by talking up his new one, who he eventually married.

"What does she do for a living?" asked the buxom blonde.

"She's a pharmacist," Donald replied.

"What's a pharmacist?" she asked.

"A farmer who wears Wellington boots," he said, deadpan.

"Oh," she nodded, apparently satisfied. We left immediately to avoid further embarrassment.

As an apprentice, you were the butt of everyone's jokes. "Go get a glass hammer," they'd say, or "fetch some tartan paint." My favourite was when they sent me to get a "long stand" from the engineers. An hour later, Donald found me sitting in the engineers' workshop, reading the paper.

"What's he doing in here?" Donald asked.

"I don't know," the engineer replied. "He came in, said you were taking the piss, and sat down."

My glasses were broken again.

The mill had proper engineers, though, and they relied on four main tools: a 2lb hammer, a 4lb hammer, a 6lb hammer, and a fire poker. You guarded your poker with your life. It was the most important tool for repairing the machines.

I eventually got my revenge on Saturday mornings. Donald would come in hungover or still drunk and head straight for the toilets with the day's newspaper. I'd run the section, but every now and then, I'd bang on the closed toilet doors, waking him and the other overlookers up. Oh, they loved that.

There were other young lads in the mill who weren't apprentices. One of them threatened me once in the warehouse for looking at him. I walked off—was it fear or common sense? I still wonder what would've happened if I had fought him and been fired. I'm not sure, but I think it was fear. It's been 48 years, and I still feel ashamed that I didn't stand up for myself. So much for living in the present.

It wasn't just the men who took the mick out of apprentices. The women had their own tricks. One day, I was waiting at the breakfast trolley for my usual cup of tea and sandwich when a new woman, small and about 40 years old, turned to me and said, "It's warm in 'ere, isn't it?"

"Yes, it is," I replied.

She unzipped her top and said, "I've got nothing under 'ere, look."

She was right—there was nothing underneath.

Another woman had a trick where she'd hold out her hand for a handshake, and when you reached for it, she'd quickly grab your tackle instead. There were also times when the women would gang up on me and take my jeans, leaving me to work in just my underpants, T-shirt, and boots. One time, a rather large woman sat on me to hold me down while the others took off my jeans. I couldn't move because of her weight. When an attractive 18-year-old did the same thing, I couldn't move for other reasons—especially with her mum watching.

After work, I'd often stop at the shop on my way home to buy a can of garden peas. With two slices of bread and some margarine, that was my tea.

Once a year, the company sent the best apprentice on an Outward-Bound course. In my first year, I was nominated, but another apprentice who had just completed his course was selected instead. I wasn't too bothered—there would be other chances. However, a week before he was due to go, he tried to jump over a garden gate while drunk and broke his leg.

On Monday, I was called into the office and told I'd be going in his place. By Friday, I was off to Eskdale in Cumbria for a three-week Outward-Bound course. They sent me to Bradford to pick up some walking boots and a rucksack, and by Thursday, I had a train ticket in hand. I had never heard of Outward Bound or Eskdale, and I had never spent more than a week away from home. To top it off, I was travelling alone—and I don't think I had ever been on a train before.

Somehow, I got there. I was in a group of 12 lads—some from the army, the gas board, Yorkshire Electricity, and other apprentices from Scotland to Hatfield. I particularly remember a guy from Hatfield called Selwyn. He arrived in a cashmere suit, good-looking, with beautifully coiffured hair—clearly a man about town. Within two weeks, he would be setting fire to the toilet paper he'd just used out in the open air on the moors.

I was the youngest there. Everyone had to sign a contract not to drink or smoke for the three weeks. I kept to it; others didn't. We mountain-climbed, camped without tents on top of mountains, canoed in the sea, orienteered, and walked across mountain ridges. The person in charge of our group was a man named Rod Pashley. One night, he told us a story about a boy with asthma who was weak and lacking in confidence and had completed the course. Of course, the boy was him. Two weeks later, as we climbed the mountains without him, we were all shouting, *"You're still an asthmatic b**d!"*

I enjoyed the whole experience, and it did give me confidence.

I liked being an apprentice. My plan was simple: go to college on day release for five years, get my Higher City and Guilds, and, in the meantime, hang out with my friends, drink, go to concerts, and not bother about much else.

After only 18 months, I was called into the office to see Alan Wright, the Mill Manager.

"Did you see that job advert for an Overlooker on the Evening Shift?"

"Yes."

"Congratulations, you got it."

"But I didn't apply."

"Tough. You start Monday at 12:45 and finish at 8:30 p.m. Tea at 4."

"But I don't want to."

"You'll be fine. Close the door on your way out. Neville, give him a new contract."

There I was, 18 years old, in my first supervisory job, in charge of five women from the estate. Worse still, one of them was my older sister!

The things we did in the mill back then would lead to disciplinaries, warnings, dismissals, or "re-education" in inclusivity, treating others with respect, and emotional intelligence today. I'm not sure which is worse. Let me correct that—I *know* what's worse. Sometimes, I long for the mill.

The Stoic philosopher and Roman emperor Marcus Aurelius addresses work in *Meditations* when he says:

> "I AM RISING TO DO THE WORK OF A HUMAN BEING. WHY THEN, AM I SO IRRITABLE IF I AM GOING OUT TO DO WHAT I WAS BORN TO DO AND WHAT I WAS BROUGHT INTO THIS WORLD FOR?
>
> (THEPHILOSOPHYOFEVERYTHING.COM)"

Marcus Aurelius is one of my favourite philosophers. He's the father of Stoic philosophy—practical, down-to-earth. He could have been a Yorkshireman.

Why do we find it difficult to motivate ourselves to do something that is natural to us? *Is it natural?*

Sigmund Freud says in *Civilization and Its Discontents* that man needs two things for happiness:

> "LOVE AND WORK, WORK AND LOVE.
>
> (THEPHILOSOPHYOFEVERYTHING.COM)"

Sir Clive Woodward, the winning manager of England's World Cup team, apparently said,

> "YOU DON'T HAVE TO GO TO WORK; YOU GET TO GO TO WORK."

I've always enjoyed work. I've always been able to get up in the morning. I'm even okay with some stress. What I *can't* take is boredom. Sometimes, I think I'm like a sheriff from the old West. I clean companies up, get rid of the baddies, bring peace and harmony, and when it gets boring, I move on. Obviously, that also means I have no patience.

I also have to admit that I have a problem with authority. If someone above me knows less than me and tries to impose their view, well, that winds me up.

The point I'm trying to make is that it's *my* career, *my* job, *my* responsibility. My biggest fear is when it's *not.* When you get dismissed or made redundant against your wishes, there's nothing you can do about it. Is it naïve to think my future is my responsibility, under my control, or is that just wishful thinking?

I've never bought into the paternal view of companies looking after their employees.

There have been studies that review companies against a psychological test, and companies nearly always come out as psychopaths. When it's in the company's interest to be nice, they can be. I've seen and attended so many events, programs, and initiatives by companies trying to make it a happy workplace. But when the going gets tough, companies act like psychopaths.

Don't get me wrong—being happy at work is important. But happiness comes from knowing what you need to do to be successful, being supported with encouragement and advice to achieve your aim and working in a profitable company. A T-shirt or pseudo-philosophical support promises much but delivers little. It's fashionable to have training courses on diversity, inclusiveness, and being supportive and caring. Better still, teach awareness and consciousness. We treat the symptom, not the cause.

There are three things I look for in a work colleague, whether they're above or beneath me:

1. *Do they look the part?* This is the least important to me, but it often matters more to higher management. They tend to want people who look and dress like them. It's about setting the example: if you want a clean, neat, and organised factory, you should look clean, neat, and organised.

2. *Do they act the part?* This is more important than simply looking the part. It's about doing what you say you'll do—not acting superior or pretending to be a leader, but actually being one. I've had bosses who thought everything that came before them was rubbish, dismissing good practices just

to prove they were in charge. The truth is, after five years, you're no longer the cure—you're either part of the problem or the success. If you act as you talk, that's a good start.

3. *Can they do the part?* This is the most critical. I can live with someone who does not look or act the part perfectly, but they must be able to *do* the part. Actually contributing positively, knowing how to create a successful and happy company, and learning from mistakes instead of covering them up or blaming others—that's what's required. Acting with integrity, praising more, and blaming less. Too many people look the part and act the part but cannot actually *do* the part.

I don't think I ever quite looked the part, but I'm not bad at the other two criteria.

Often, though, it's the people who look and talk the part who progress. *Promote your mistakes,* they used to say. It's a great way to piss everyone else off.

I've worked for some great MDs, Chairmen, and Directors. But I've also worked for some fools. This isn't a moan—no, really—it's just how it is. What the people in charge *should* want is staff who support them but also challenge the status quo to improve things. Too often, though, managers are more interested in maintaining their perceived status. They take "management decisions" against anyone who disagrees with them, stifling progress to protect their own standing. It's what I call *Waking Sleep*—not just for themselves, but for everyone around them. Their main purpose is maintaining or increasing their status.

I've come across many people who've stayed with the same company, climbed the corporate ladder, and eventually found themselves trapped in roles beyond their actual capabilities. They can never leave because they've been promoted too far beyond their competence.

> COMPANIES EITHER GO FORWARD OR BACKWARDS; THEY NEVER STAY STILL.
>
> DAVID MIDGLEY

Promoting beyond capability is a sure way of going backwards. Yet, due to status, discrimination (of all kinds), and self-interest, this happens a lot.

I have opinions, but I base most of my decisions on facts and data. My approach to achieving the best outcomes for both people and the company has been shaped by years of both failures and successes. I don't always agree with management—and that's why I've been sacked twice.

Indecision and prevarication help no one. However, if someone has an idea that, after analysis, is better than mine, I'll drop my idea and *steal* theirs—ensuring they get the credit, of course.

Steal with pride.

David, stop digressing. *Is work natural?* Yes, I think so.

I'm a big fan of Maslow's Hierarchy of Needs.

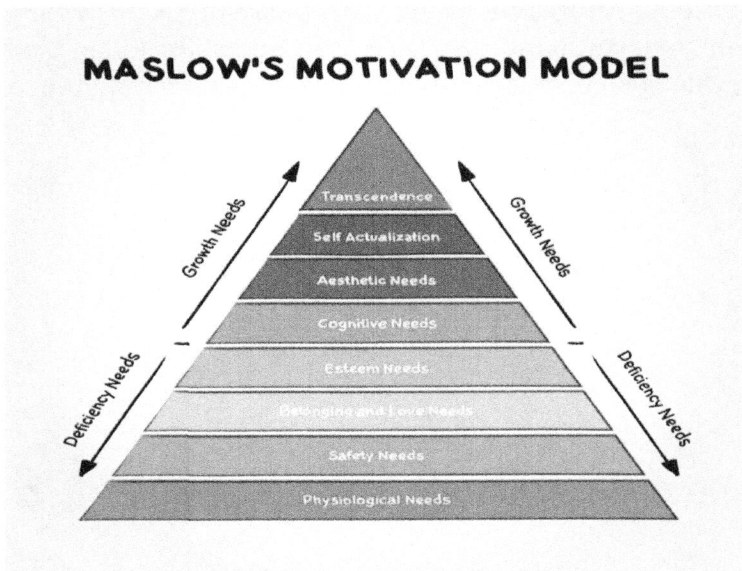

Simply Psychology.com

Let me translate *Maslow's Hierarchy of Needs* into Yorkshire terms:

- **Physiological Needs**: Having enough money to go to the chippy and the pub. Work helps provide these.

- **Safety Needs**: Having somewhere to sleep without getting wet. You pay for that through work.

- **Belonging and Love Needs**: Having a wife and kids, putting food on the table.
- **Esteem**: Having mates—people who respect you.
- **Cognitive Needs**: Knowing who you are.
- **Aesthetic Needs**: Knowing what you like, appreciating the talent of others, and being moved by it.
- **Self-Actualization**: Understanding yourself and others.
- **Transcendence**: Using that understanding for the good of others.

The early parts of this hierarchy—your basic needs—can only really be achieved through work. The higher levels are about understanding yourself and your place in the world.

And what if I didn't work? I could live off the grid, grow crops, or turn to crime.

No, I couldn't. Someone owns that field, and everything still needs paying for. I once stole a packet of crisps at school and felt so bad I threw them away. That was the end of my criminal career.

Work helps fulfil those basic needs. The quality and amount of what I want determines how much or how hard I need to work. But don't forget—work isn't there on Christmas Day.

I've fallen into the trap of putting work before family in the past, and I've paid for it. I've been asked to leave companies due to internal politics, fear, and power struggles. I tied my self-esteem to my job, and without the job, I felt like I had no self-esteem. I was wrong, but at the time, it didn't feel that way.

It's tough to learn, but a good way to look at things is: *"Do your best and let go of the outcome."*

I don't know where that saying came from, but it's true—and incredibly hard to do.

CHAPTER FIVE

BACK TO THE MILL, GETTING MARRIED, AND MUSIC

The ladies I supervised worked from 4:30 to 8:30 p.m., Monday to Friday. They were there for what we called "pin money"—to help with household bills, to get away from the kids and husband, or for some social interaction. At least one woman would often show up smelling of Australian white wine, which was sold cheaply at the local off-licence. But generally, they were a good group.

My section was the furthest from the clocking-out machine, and queues started forming at 8:20 p.m. I wouldn't let my ladies head to the machine until 8:25. They didn't like it at first, but bit by bit, I won them over by helping out—keeping the machines running if they needed the toilet or unloading heavy tops from the carts they were working on.

Inside the mill, there were designated smoking areas close to the machines. If the gilling machine broke down, the women would lift the top cover to signal me that it was out of order and then head off to the smoke table. The worst one for this habit was my older sister.

For revenge, I'd take out all 74 fallers—metal combs with inch-long sharp teeth—and tell her to come back and clean them. These were wrapped tightly in wool or polyester and were tough to clean. Cuts and pricks were normal. I'd always beckoned her over with my index finger. Of course, she'd go home and tell our mother that I was picking on her, which I was. But what happens at work stays at work.

I did enjoy the Overlookers' work trips, though. Every week, we'd each put £1 into a kitty for our yearly day out. It was men-only, of course, and we usually chose between Blackpool, Scarborough, York, Bridlington, or, if we were feeling adventurous, Morecambe.

Being the youngest ever Overlooker and surrounded by middle-aged men, I asked if my mate Steve could join us. Even after I left the company, Steve and I kept going on these trips. Eventually, Steve had been on more trips than nearly anyone else, and he'd never even worked for the company!

Some highlights include us knocking on pub doors at 10:30 in the morning in Bridlington, begging to be let in. Or apprentice Andy getting so drunk in the Manchester pub in Blackpool that he fell on his back and kept talking, not realising he'd fallen—even though beer was pouring over his chest.

These were the days when pubs shut at 3 p.m. and didn't reopen until 5 p.m., so by mid-afternoon, we were usually plastered. One time, we were playing football on the beach in Scarborough, barefoot, when apprentice Andy broke Overlooker Steve's toe. Steve didn't feel it much at the time, but the next day, once sober, he had to go to the hospital. Another memorable moment was going on the Waltzers at Blackpool's Pleasure Beach, where the operator kept spinning our car as fast as he could, trying to make us sick. *Happy times.*

Morecambe was another good trip. Steve and I got on the "Wild Mouse" ride, thinking it looked pretty tame.

"This doesn't look like much," I said drunkenly.

"You don't know what's wrong with it," said the operator and pulled the lever.

"Shit!" I was saved from seeing much of the ride by Steve's long hair, which kept flapping in my face.

On the way home from that trip, it was dark and rainy as we drove through the dales. Everyone was drunk, and in the back seat, Overlooker John was vomiting into a bucket we kept for such emergencies. Unfortunately, his false teeth fell into the bucket. To avoid embarrassment, he quickly fished them out and popped them back into his mouth. Everyone who saw this immediately started retching, and soon, there was a small tidal wave of vomit rolling down the centre of the bus. As the coach went downhill, the wave rushed forward, and as we went uphill, it receded. I can still smell it.

Another time, we were in York, drinking at the *Three Tuns*. There were about five of us in a narrow pub when I noticed a bottle fly through the air, followed by a chair going the other way. We quickly exited to the opposite side of the street. Two gangs appeared—one from Leeds and the other from York. There was the usual shouting and posturing, and then a small guy came out of the pub and punched someone from the other gang with a sickening crunch. We all cringed and looked away. Just then, a police van pulled up, and about four officers jumped out, looking like they were straight out of a Batman movie. The gangs scattered. We stayed put, minding our own business with our pints.

A policeman came up to us and said, *"If you don't get back in the pub, you'll be arrested for drinking in the street."* We protested, *"Hold on, those lads were about to kill each other!"*

"Any argument, and you're in the van."

We trooped back into the pub. The police left, and a few minutes later, the two gangs started filtering back in—this time, arm in arm, offering each other pints. The two lads who had been fighting were now sharing drinks as if nothing had happened. Welcome to Yorkshire.

One of the friends I made at Bulmer's was "Hairy Andy." We called him that to differentiate him from "Big Andy" from the CLB and apprentice Andy, who earned his nickname from constantly spilling drinks down his front. Hairy Andy was another Overlooker from an adjacent department. He was a little older than me and into motorbikes and music. We'd have tea together at 6 p.m. in the warehouse, which had a door to my section and one to his. Woe betide anyone, be it women or management, who dared to disturb our 20-minute tea break.

Hairy Andy joined the core group of mates—Steve, Big Andy, Tom (whose real name was Peter, but was called Tom because he was like a tomcat with women), and me.

We became a tight-knit group who regularly went out drinking.

After finishing all my City and Guilds exams and courses, I have been at Bulmer's for six years. I started to feel the desire to get my degree—just to see if I could do it. When I asked Bulmer's, they said no. They felt I had been trained enough, and no one had ever gone on to take a degree. But the thought of doing the same job for the rest of my life didn't sit well with me. So, I left and joined Interface, a mile down the road, as a laboratory technician on shifts.

I left for less money, but they agreed to pay for my degree and paid me while I studied. By then, I was married with a house. I couldn't really afford to leave Bulmer's, but I did it anyway. I can't remember having any doubts—I just did it.

I had met my first wife in a heavy rock nightclub in Halifax called *The Tramshed.* I had been drinking all weekend and spent the night headbanging, wearing an Afghan waistcoat with nothing underneath. I *loved* that waistcoat. I spotted a girl who looked completely out of place in a bright yellow disco jumpsuit. "I like your waistcoat," she said. We started snogging, and that was that. Within two years, we were married and living in a street-lined terraced house on Salterhebble Hill in Halifax.

The house cost £4,750. Her mother gave us £500 for the deposit, but I had to sign a promissory note saying that if we split up, I'd pay the money back. My wife was an 18-year-old art student in Halifax, and I was 21, living away from home for the first time. I remember our first day living together—we had a major row over how to wash clothes. I was still going out with my mates on Thursdays or Fridays and playing football on Sundays. I wasn't a great husband.

One night, after being out with my mates, I came home to find her crying because I'd left her alone for too long. The next day, I arranged the wedding at a church and told her a week later.

I had three stag nights.

The first was the traditional one around Halifax with mates and work colleagues. I tried to stay sober, and fortunately, no one tied me to any lamp posts.

The second night was with the women I supervised. They got their revenge for all the times I made them clean the fallers. After work, they dragged me to the pub and plied me with gin and orange—about 12 in two hours. I avoided pints because I had to catch the bus and didn't want to need the loo. I was hammered. When I met my fiancée, I was sitting on a wall near the hospital, vomiting so hard I fell over backwards, producing a fountain of sick.

The last one was the night before the wedding. Steve, my brother Ian (who was the best man), and Dave Crossley from my CLB days were staying at my house, while my fiancée stayed at her mum's. "Let's go for a couple down the local," Steve suggested. At this point, Steve had an optic attached to a bottle of whiskey over his pillow at home, so I should've known better. We went out and got hammered—again. Especially my brother, who could barely stand.

We got married in a church, and it was a good day, though the reception at Leeds Road Community Centre in Halifax was a bit of a letdown. The DJ didn't turn up, but my wife looked great. We had a coach from Buttershaw for family and friends. Most of the men disappeared for two hours to a local pub because the beer was better. My brother Ian was one of them.

Throughout these years, from apprentice to Overlooker and even after getting married, I kept going to college one day and evening a week. On the first day, I met two guys who became firm friends, and we often participated in the *Tetley Pub Hunts*. You'd get a card at the pub for every pint you drank, stamped with the pub's name. Once you had a stamp from 10 different pubs, you could send it off for a free T-shirt. When the event was on, we'd spend most of our lunchtimes trying to get those stamps.

One time, I got so drunk I had to go home and miss some of my college classes. Halfway home, in Queensbury, I had to get off the bus for a piss. I had long hair and was wearing my favourite denim jacket. When I got home, my wife opened the door to find me with vomit in my hair and dripping down my jacket. To be fair, she laughed and took it well. I never washed that jacket—I kept it for years, with mould growing on it.

The house we lived in had four floors and sat on a steep hill. We stayed there for 13 years, trying to make it a home. We had some good parties, and I still remember ripping out the '50s fireplace (which is apparently back in demand now) with the back boiler while watching *Live Aid*. It was our first home, and looking back, I was naïve, young, and a bit selfish. It was two bus rides to Bulmer's and only slightly closer to Interface. I woke at 05:00 am to walk into Halifax for 05:45 am to catch the bus to Interface.

We got by, but with my wife not earning money while she was still at college, things were tight. Yet, despite the financial strain, I moved on from Bulmer's as a Supervisor to Interface as a Quality Controller on double day shifts. Something kept driving me forward, but I still don't know what.

Adventures in Music

> PHILOSOPHY IS THE HIGHEST MUSIC.
>
> MUSIC IS A MORAL LAW. IT GIVES A SOUL TO THE UNIVERSE, WINGS TO THE MIND, FLIGHT TO THE IMAGINATION, A CHARM TO SADNESS, GAIETY AND LIFE TO EVERYTHING. IT IS THE ESSENCE OF ORDER, AND LEADS TO ALL THAT IS GOOD AND JUST AND BEAUTIFUL.
>
> PLATO

It was around this time, 1980... wow, such a long time ago, that I really started getting into music. The first two albums I bought were *Venus and Mars* by Wings and *The Original Soundtrack* by 10cc. But one Sunday afternoon, I was at Steve's parents' house when he handed me a headset and said, *"Put this on and listen to this."*

Heavy rock music shot through my ears like lightning, crashing into my brain. I loved it. It was *If You Want Blood*, a live AC/DC album. After that, I decided to grow my hair out.

My first major concert was at St. George's Hall, where I saw Def Leppard, supported by Magnum. Magnum were great; Def Leppard, less so. After that, Steve, Hairy Andy, Tom, and I went to tons of concerts. Mostly, it was Steve and me: AC/DC, Levellers, Motorhead, UFO, Whitesnake, Scorpions, Saxon, Rush—back in the early '80s, during the NWOBHM (*New Wave of British Heavy Metal*). Every week, there was a band to see. We were founding members of the mosh pit.

We heard about a rock club at the Princeville Working Men's Club in Bradford. We went, loved it, and joined that first night. Every Thursday, we'd see bands like Chevy, Diamond Head, Limelight, and many others of varying quality. Often, they were supported by the Chaos Brothers, who were like DJs with cardboard guitars and flash bombs on their hats.

The club was loud. We were amazed by this old man gathering glasses in a white jacket, casually walking in front of the stage, seemingly unaffected by the music. Then we noticed he had cotton wool stuffed in his ears.

Sundays were reserved for *Rockers and Knockers*—a stripper would perform before and after the band. Most of the time, the strippers didn't turn up. Either they couldn't find the place, or they thought better of it.

Once, *Sounds* magazine came to report on a band called Silverwing, who were supposed to be the next big thing. They were awful. The audience booed them off the stage after about five songs. The magazine later wrote that Bradford liked its music: heavy and fast. Yep, that sounded about right.

My first trip abroad was to see AC/DC in Brussels. Steve and I were at the Princeville when we saw an advert in *Sounds* for the trip. It was Thursday, the trip was on Saturday, and the concert was on Sunday night. Steve looked at me, I looked at him, and we said, *"Let's do it."*

The next morning, we booked the trip, went to the post office to get our paper passports (remember those?), and that Friday night, we caught the overnight coach to London.

We barely made it onto the coach in time. At the back were lads from Glasgow, at the front were Londoners, and Steve and I sat in the middle. The coach had to stop a few times after the ferry because everyone was drinking heavily. It was during this trip that I learned *"prive"* meant *private*, not a toilet as I'd thought.

That night, I got dressed in a suit for a night out in Brussels. I went downstairs, only to find everyone in jeans and T-shirts. I quickly changed into jeans, an AC/DC T-shirt, and a black jacket. I looked great with long hair and a flat cap. Two Londoners asked to join us, figuring safety in numbers, one of whom was nicknamed Piglet.

We found a bar where all the Glasgow lads were. They quickly came over and told the bar staff that they were the road crew—and that we were AC/DC. The Londoners couldn't understand a word the Glaswegians said, but we played along and got free drinks for the rest of the night. Back at the hotel, drunk, the Glasgow lads suggested we re-enact the Battle of Bannockburn. No problem. They threw spotlights at us, and we hurled whatever we could find back at them until the hotel manager threatened to kick us all out.

The Sunday night concert was incredible. AC/DC were brilliant—it was their last show in Europe on the *Back in Black* tour. After the concert, it was straight back onto the coach for the ferry home. Onboard, we saw the real AC/DC road crew sitting on the roadside, drinking Jack Daniel's after a long tour.

While waiting for the bus home in London, Steve and I fell asleep on the grass outside Buckingham Palace.

Over the years, we've been to hundreds of concerts. I still remember one trip to see AC/DC in Birmingham, where I tried (and failed) to piss into an empty milk bottle on the coach. Everyone on board was laughing at me. Then there was Judas Priest in Sheffield. Hairy Andy drove his van, and Steve and I drank every can of strong lager we could find in the back. Steve passed out and missed the entire concert.

At a Gillan concert at St. George's, we had the best seats in the house in the dress circle. But we were so drunk we could hardly move for fear of being sick.

We also went to the first-ever *Monsters of Rock* at Donington. The coach driver told us he'd be leaving at 10:30 p.m. We laughed. The concert finished at 11 p.m., and when we got back to the coach park, it was empty. Thousands of people were wandering around, wondering where their buses had gone. We eventually made it to Derby train station, which looked like a scene from *Gone with the Wind*—bodies sprawled everywhere, but instead of Confederate uniforms, they wore black leather jackets. We finally caught the early train back to Bradford, though not to the usual Interchange station—this time, it was the little-used Forster Square station. Steve woke up, saw a cage marked *"Bristol"*, screamed, and I pretended to wake up and scream too.

One year, we went to *Monsters of Rock* on a local pub trip. It was the first time I saw someone light a fart and actually create flames.

The Levellers at York Barbican was another standout concert. We spent all day drinking in York. Usually, the warm-up music is forgettable, but this time, they played *Never Mind the Bollocks* by the Sex Pistols. The crowd sang along to *"Anarchy in the UK"*, and when the Levellers came on, it was electric. I lost Steve during the show, but when it was over, we stood smiling at each other. We've seen the Levellers many times since. Most recently, my good friend Neil took me to see them for my 60th birthday. The usual chaos ensued—people getting thrown out, police in the toilets, paramedics—but afterwards, we left the anarchist concert and stepped into a stretch limo to take us home. Times have changed.

I still go to concerts, but these days, it's more likely to be Kate Rusby or Paul Carrick. Some of the great bands still tour, but when you see Angus with white hair, Lemmy is now dead, Ozzy stumbling, and Phil Collins and Brian Johnson going deaf, I think I'd rather remember them in their heyday.

“

MUSIC IS A HIGHER REVELATION THAN ALL WISDOM AND PHILOSOPHY.

LUDWIG VAN BEETHOVEN

”

What made me love it so much? Burning off nervous energy was definitely part of it. But there was also something spiritual about it. Listening to *Supper's Ready* by Genesis with Peter Gabriel still sends tingles through my brain. Heavy rock—especially at a live concert—can give such peace of mind; it's like meditation. It soothes like an Aloe Vera wrap.

“

LIFE WITHOUT MUSIC IS A MISTAKE.

FRIEDRICH NIETZSCHE

”

CHAPTER SIX

ADVENTURES AT INTERFACE AND SOCIETY

I joined Interface Flooring Systems in Shelf, Halifax, and stayed with them for 10 years. They made carpet tiles and had recently been bought by an American company. I was promoted twice, starting as a shift Quality Controller and eventually becoming the Product Development Manager. Over time, the wages improved, and with the promotions, I was able to buy a semi-detached bungalow in a nice area of Queensbury. My wife and I also had a lovely child.

Sounds good, doesn't it?

But this is where I think the wheels began to fall off. I started being careful about what I said and entered the world of office politics and the upper-working-class banality. Of course, there were still the odd slip-ups.

"I want an electrician," said a female operative.

"You might as well; you've had everyone else," I quipped.

An hour later, her husband, who also worked there, confronted me face to face: *"I will bury an axe in your head."*

"If you were going to do that, you already would have", I replied

I had to apologise to her in front of the Operations Director.

Then there was the time a lady from marketing called me, and I answered, *"David Midgley at your cervix."*

But I didn't get everything wrong. I'd only been at Interface a week when I was walking with the new chemist, who had joined on the same day as me. We had gone to school together, so we knew each other. Across the yard, we saw two people walking up the hill—Keith, one of our colleagues in the lab, and Basil, the Operations Director. "Hi, Keith," I called out. The chemist, eager to please, yelled, *"Hello, Basil!"*

From that day on, I was known as "okay," while the chemist was labelled a brown nose. It stayed that way for the next 10 years.

Keith, a funny bloke that he was, had a stash of *Sadie Stern* female domination magazines hidden in the experimental shed. Great guy, but a bit odd. When he left the company for a competitor, he launched a product range called "Banker."

"Wanker," muttered Bob Mantle, my boss and the Technical Manager, who sadly passed away some years ago.

The chemist had started at a higher grade than me—he was a qualified chemist, after all, while I was textiles-trained. But things didn't work out for him, and he stayed at his grade while I rose through the ranks. He became the butt of some hard jokes. Once, we primed a committed Christian named Roger to join in when we all pretended to hate the chemist. The whole scene was planned and executed—though not by me but by another lab rat named Dave.

"I hate you," said Dave.

"Funny that, I hate you too," I added.

The chemist, looking defeated, turned to Roger: *"You don't hate me, do you, Roger? You're a Christian."*

Roger, to his credit, played along: *"Yes, I hate you as well."*

The chemist turned and walked away, devastated. It was only after I chased him down to explain that we were just messing with him that he calmed down. But I didn't sleep for a few nights after that. It wasn't the heat of the moment that bothered me—it was the fact that it had all been planned. I couldn't cope with that.

Another lesson learned.

We always worked on Christmas Eve and went to the pub at lunchtime. One Christmas, I had too much to drink and introduced a colleague to my wife as "Steve stab-you-in-the-back Martin." It wasn't funny, it wasn't true, and it was hurtful. I didn't sleep all Christmas. "Don't be a dick" is good advice, and I wasn't following it.

I apologised after the holidays, but I realised that my sarcasm, my mouth, was taking me places I didn't want to go. I was losing control, so I started to become quieter and quieter.

I eventually passed my degree—two afternoons and evenings a week for four years—and then enrolled in a Diploma in Management Studies at Bradford. My wife asked me not to because we had just had a child, but I had to challenge myself. So I did it. I wasn't a good husband.

The course group was a great bunch, mostly from the council, and we'd go out drinking after class. One evening, during a particularly lively debate, someone turned to me and said, *"You need to get a personality—you never challenge anything!"*

Me? No personality?

Looking back now, I can see that I was torn between wanting to fit into society and the desire to smash it to pieces. I had become risk-averse—afraid of being reported at work, afraid of not being liked. Yet, underneath it all, I was frustrated, angry, and longing for adventure. Everything felt like it was pressing down on me, except for one thing—my daughter.

Philosophy and Society

Society
/'sə'sīədē/

> "A COMMUNITY, NATION, OR BROAD GROUPING OF PEOPLE HAVING COMMON TRADITIONS, INSTITUTIONS, AND COLLECTIVE ACTIVITIES AND INTERESTS.
>
> MERRIAM WEBSTER"

My view of society is... complicated. In no particular order:

- Society allows wars.
- Society votes Tory/Reform.
- Society votes Brexit.
- Society promotes prejudice.
- Society promotes division in wealth, education, and religion.
- Society's hidden rules about what's acceptable and what's not are a method of control that I reject.

"

OUR SOCIETY IS RUN BY INSANE PEOPLE FOR INSANE OBJECTIVES. I THINK WE'RE BEING RUN BY MANIACS FOR MANIACAL ENDS, AND I THINK I'M LIABLE TO BE PUT AWAY AS INSANE FOR EXPRESSING THAT. THAT'S WHAT'S INSANE ABOUT IT.

JOHN LENNON (BRAINYQUOTE.COM)

"

"

THE TROUBLE WITH THE RAT RACE IS THAT EVEN IF YOU WIN, YOU'RE STILL A RAT.

LILY TOMLIN (BRAINYQUOTE.COM)

"

I started realising that society, with all its rules, structures, and expectations, felt like a trap. At Interface, I had a good job, a house, a family—but I also had a gnawing sense that none of it truly mattered. I was navigating office politics and the social expectations that came with climbing the corporate ladder, but something felt off.

At times, I wanted to blow it all up, tear down the system that made me play it safe, keep quiet, and toe the line. Yet, at the same time, I feared stepping out of line, feared what it might cost me. This tension, between the desire to belong and the urge to rebel, shaped much of how I navigated my career and my place in society.

As you can see, I'm not a great believer in society, but for now, this society is all we have. History isn't littered with better alternatives for governance.

There are many good things about our society. First, it could be worse. For all our issues, we generally don't kill each other *too* much, and I do believe that people genuinely want to be good.

Do we need society?

> HE WHO IS UNABLE TO LIVE IN SOCIETY, OR WHO HAS NO NEED BECAUSE HE IS SUFFICIENT FOR HIMSELF, MUST BE EITHER A BEAST OR A GOD.
>
> ARISTOTLE (BRAINYQUOTE.COM)

It's very hard to live without society, and it can be lonely.

> THE INDIVIDUAL HAS ALWAYS HAD TO STRUGGLE TO KEEP FROM BEING OVERWHELMED BY THE TRIBE. IF YOU TRY IT, YOU WILL BE LONELY OFTEN, AND SOMETIMES FRIGHTENED. BUT NO PRICE IS TOO HIGH TO PAY FOR THE PRIVILEGE OF OWNING YOURSELF.
>
> FRIEDRICH NIETZSCHE (PINTEREST.COM)

Wise words. It's a lonely existence to always plough your own furrow. We're brought up to work, find someone, get married, have children, own a home, and die peacefully, surrounded by friends and family.

Or, in other words: be born, live in *Waking Sleep*, and lie on your deathbed wondering, *"Was that it?"*

Shakespeare had his own thoughts on life:

> ALL THE WORLD'S A STAGE,
> AND ALL THE MEN AND WOMEN MERELY PLAYERS;
> THEY HAVE THEIR EXITS AND THEIR ENTRANCES,
> AND ONE MAN IN HIS TIME PLAYS MANY PARTS,
> HIS ACTS BEING SEVEN AGES...
>
> SHAKESPEARE, WIKIPEDIA

There are billions of people on this planet. Do we all have to follow the same path? Mostly, yes. Are we expected to? To some degree, we are. That's what society demands.

But what do we really want for our children? If it's not this, then what is life for?

IT IS NO MEASURE OF HEALTH TO BE WELL ADJUSTED TO A PROFOUNDLY SICK SOCIETY.

J. KRISHNAMURTI (GOODREADS.COM)

If society is sick, what can we do?

ALL THAT IS VALUABLE IN HUMAN SOCIETY DEPENDS UPON THE OPPORTUNITY FOR DEVELOPMENT ACCORDED THE INDIVIDUAL.

ALBERT EINSTEIN (BRAINYQUOTE.COM)

Individual opportunity—provided by society. Is it true?

Yes. But do we believe in it? Do we even recognise an opportunity when we see one? I, for one, cannot take a hint.

Is it my nature or nurture that makes me sceptical of past, present, and future society? I was 17 or 18, walking to Queensbury from Buttershaw on a Sunday with Big Andy. At the time, I had been involved with the WRP and Young Socialists for a couple of years. Maggie had just gotten back in for her second term as prime minister, and Big Andy asked me why I looked so sad.

I told him, *"Because Maggie's back in power, and she's done nothing for the poor or disadvantaged."*

I remember saying, *"Sod it. This society is crap. The only way to survive it is to make as much money as you can, and then get the fuck out of it."*

Andy, strong as he was, put me on his shoulders, and we walked the rest of the way up hill to Queensbury.

Not long after that, I left the WRP/YS. That thought—make money, then get out—has stayed with me ever since, even though I never made enough to achieve it.

I talked about *Waking Sleep* earlier, and I believe that's what society is. Millions of people walking around in a daydream. The society we've created allows us to live in that dream without ever really waking up. In fact, most people are afraid of waking up.

But sometimes, things happen. Is it universal consciousness, God, nature, or society itself that creates moments to wake us up? Wars, epidemics, famine, the loss of a job, divorce, bereavement—all these can make us stop and think: *Is this it?*

How does society respond to these challenges? Mostly with indifference, until it's forced to act. It takes a lot to wake society up.

Hitler, for example, told everyone what he was going to do in *Mein Kampf*. Once in power, he took over Austria, the Sudetenland, and Czechoslovakia, and then set his sights on Poland—exactly as he'd said he would.

The lesson here: if someone says that a particular group of people is the root of all evil and they get into power, what do you think is going to happen?

What *did* happen? World War II and the Holocaust.

The U.S. took three years to wake up to this. Isolationism equals *Waking Sleep*.

More recently, everyone could see COVID coming over the hill from China, but governments only acted when people started dying. They were in *Waking Sleep*.

African countries would stand a much better chance of avoiding famine if they didn't have to repay the loans given to them by the countries and societies that exploited them in the first place. Who's asleep now?

Governments focus on short-term issues to ensure they get re-elected.

> “DON'T MAKE SHORT-TERM DECISIONS AGAINST LONG-TERM GOALS.
>
> LEAN PHILOSOPHY”

As I write this, Hamas has launched a surprise attack on Israel, killing civilians. This is terrible and cannot be justified. But neither can the treatment of Palestinians over decades by the Israeli government. What has society done about that? Very little. Israel is pro-West, supported by wealthy Americans, and the cycle continues.

So, what can we do? Is there an issue with society?

My conclusions, after talking it through with the wife (my Penelope), are that society's biggest problem is how it views itself.

When society becomes inward-looking, separating itself from other cultures, religions, perspectives, and nations, it stops thinking about what's right philosophically. Instead, it gets stuck in the past or lost in dreams of the future, submerged in *Waking Sleep*. And that's the real problem: separation. Separation leads to fear, fear leads to hate—or, perhaps worse, to indifference.

When society becomes exclusive—defining itself by what it is *not* and excluding those who are different—it starts to stagnate. A society that only allows belonging if others don't, becomes like a still pond, and still ponds fester.

What we need is a society that's inclusive. We should respect our own traditions, yes, but we should also respect others' traditions—ones that can add good ideas and foster joint learning.

Am I starting to sound like a hippy? *Man.*

I have no time for cultures that discriminate based on colour or gender to exert power. That's not culture; it's fear and exploitation.

I'm a proud Yorkshireman (well, who wouldn't be?), but I have no problem with proud Frenchmen, Germans, Scots, or even Lancastrians (except, of course, those who support Salford United—most of them live in the South anyway).

So yes, as Shakespeare said, there are stages of life most people go through. But those stages don't need to define us, nor should they make us slaves to society.

Treat society as the necessary structure that it is, but don't let it put you to sleep. Stand aside from it and review it.

Osho said:

> “THERE IS NO NEED TO SEEK A PHILOSOPHY OF LIFE; LIFE IS ENOUGH. ALL PHILOSOPHIES ARE FALSE, INCLUDING MY PHILOSOPHY. WHEN I SAY ALL, I MEAN ALL.
>
> WAKE UP! PLEASE WAKE UP! THAT'S ALL THAT CAN BE SAID”

We're no better or worse than anyone else. If you want to change society, start by changing yourself. Don't give in to fear or prejudice. Don't fall asleep. Be the society you wish it to be.

Footnote

I was discussing this subject with two of my best friends over a bottle—or three—of wine. I was taken aback when they both agreed that society is crap. Each of them shared a moral dilemma they'd recently experienced.

One story involved Mike and his wife, who were sitting by the fire on a cold night in the pub. A large group of beaters (from the local shoot, mostly women) came in. They hadn't booked the room but wanted to sit together. They had a table booked later in the restaurant, but since Mike and his wife didn't move from their spot by the fire, one of the women remarked loudly to her friend that they couldn't sit together because Mike's wife was being "rude." Mike, who is currently recovering from a heart attack, had his evening ruined by the comment.

The other story involved Neil. He was in another pub (yes, I know the company I keep) hosting a women's Rugby Union meal. The women were watching a Rugby Union game on TV when the local football fan walked in, as he did every week, to watch the football match. He was a regular; the women were not. Without hesitation, he switched the channel to the football, much to the dismay of the women and the landlord.

Both of my friends used these examples to illustrate what they thought was wrong with society.

But who was wrong, and who was right?

We came to the conclusion that everyone sees themselves as having certain rights, and they feel compelled to defend those rights: the right to *first come, first served* by the fire, the right of a regular in a pub versus those who come irregularly.

What's missing is consideration for others.

Both scenarios reflect this tension between inclusivity and exclusivity. The couple by the fire excluded the group of beaters. The rugby team excluded the football fans. And yet, the beaters could have gathered around the couple, and the football fan could have moved to another room.

The core issue? They didn't consider the situation from the other's point of view. If they had seen their neighbour in themselves, there wouldn't have been an issue.

Where do we start? With ourselves. That doesn't mean giving in to others; it means seeing things as they truly are and acting accordingly. When you act with the best intentions for everyone and let go of the outcome, things *will* improve.

Back to Interface

There were many good things about Interface. The senior management were generally decent people who genuinely tried to do their best. The Managing Director proudly wore his Yorkshire cricket tie, priding himself on "playing life with a straight bat." Basil, the Operations Director, never lost his temper and spent a lot of time on the shop floor, which I respected.

When I became the Product Development Manager, I needed to recruit an assistant. I chose a young woman who seemed to have the right attitude. *Attitude combined with intelligence is everything.* She started on the 2nd of January.

"Did you have a good Christmas?" I asked.

"I don't celebrate Christmas," she replied.

Hello, I thought *this is interesting.*

"I'm a Jehovah's Witness," she added.

She hadn't mentioned that in the job interview (and nor should she have), but I was intrigued. I spent the next year trying to understand the religion. Jehovah's Witnesses are often disliked for door-knocking, their separateness from society, their refusal of blood transfusions, and the belief that only a chosen few get to go to heaven.

My half-sister was also a Jehovah's Witness, and I had spent some time with her, so I already had some exposure to the faith. But as I got to know this young woman, some colleagues began to suspect I was considering becoming one myself. I explored the religion out of curiosity, but I found it wanting. People like to label you, to fit you into neat categories. (Am I doing the same now by labelling others? See what I mean about disappearing up your own arse)

The truth is, there are countless ways to interpret the Bible, and this was just one of them. What struck me most was that there was little room for critique or questioning within their belief system. You're either all in, or you're not. That approach doesn't work for me. I've never been able to just accept direction—I need to challenge it, test it, see if it holds up.

It's probably a flaw of mine that I've always struggled with authority. Or is it?

Jehovah's Witnesses don't promote violence. They accept all races and nationalities. But, I had issues with their views on women and the absolute rejection of same-sex relationships. Their teachings, set out over a hundred years ago in America, just didn't sit right with me. (Maybe I'm prejudiced against certain aspects of American culture. Oh well.)

In the end, the exploration satisfied my quest for meaning for a while, but I moved on.

Rising Through the Ranks

I started at Interface as a Shift Quality Controller, and within six months, I was promoted to Foreman. A year later, I became Product Development Manager.

I had what many would consider a good life: a detached bungalow, a wife, a child, and work that took me around Europe and the U.S. I had a degree and was working on my Management Diploma, all paid for by my company. On the surface, everything was great.

But I felt frustrated. And I didn't know why.

I stayed at Interface for ten years, but eventually, the frustration led me to start looking at other jobs. One opportunity was in the Northeast, in a place optimistically called New York. I went through the usual interviews and tests. (Apparently, during one interview, I spent the entire time with my trouser zip undone, and when asked where I lived, I said, "up't mountain.")

I met the company's new MD at Hartshead Moor Services. He was an ex-Dorma Marketing Director, and he certainly looked the part—smartly dressed, with a nice smile. A few weeks later, the job offer came through: Customer Services Manager, with the potential to become the General Manager. I was 33.

At last, a proper adventure—moving to Newcastle, a new life, new challenges.

My wife said, *"Don't leave me up there."* I said, *"Let's go."*

But eventually, I did leave her there. I was not a good husband.

Three months later, in October, I found myself dressed in a new suit, shivering against the cold, suitcase in hand, standing at Bradford Interchange, waiting for the train to Newcastle.

CHAPTER SEVEN

HOBART ROSE AND THE BEGINNING OF THE END —OR WAS IT THE START?

The company was called Hobart Rose. David Rose, the owner, had kept it afloat despite years of financial losses, thanks to his successful car franchises. His heart, however, was in textiles. He spent most of his time buying and selling material and part-owned a factory in China that produced cushions, curtains, and bean bags for Debenhams, IKEA, Co-ops, and designer shops.

It was a sewing company, so the workforce was predominantly women. All the male managers were addressed by their surnames: Mr. Selkeld, Mr. Williams, and so on. When they asked me what I should be called, I said, "Dave—or complete bastard, take your pick."

People were surprised to see me. The management had told everyone I was coming from Bradford, so they assumed I was Black.

I took over from a consultant director. The most memorable thing about him was that he had created a process map for his wife to follow when cooking Christmas dinner. I'm sure she appreciated that.

Six months in, the Production, Finance, and Warehouse Managers were sacked in one day, and I became the General Manager of Operations. A year later, I found myself in a pub in Cullercoats, near Tynemouth, sitting with a Manager. He was telling me that he had fallen in love with another woman who lived in Manchester. She had a child and wanted nothing to do with him, yet he was completely besotted. After an hour of listening to his story, he looked at me, crestfallen, and asked, *"What do you think?"*

After a brief pause for reflection, I replied, *"Job's fucked."* There you go—philosophy at its finest. The point is that you can apply philosophy as much as you want, but sometimes, you just have to draw a line and move on.

The company was struggling financially. We usually finished early on Fridays, with just a few Customer Service staff manning the phones. One Friday afternoon, the MD came to see me and told me the company didn't have enough money to pay staff wages the next day. At the time, we were issuing delivery notes with the works order to streamline the process. I gathered all the delivery notes from the factory, and the company posted them as delivered.

The company was operating on a "factoring" system, where whatever invoices were posted would yield 80% of their value the next day. This was just enough to cover wages.

It was bending the law to its fullest. Any invoices we couldn't fulfil were immediately credited, which caused chaos for the next two weeks—but people got paid.

Why did I do it? If I hadn't, no one would have been paid (including me), and the company would have likely closed, making everyone redundant. Did I worry about it? Yes.

The production system was based on high-volume manufacturing, but most of our orders were small and varied. We couldn't get orders out while putting large volumes of the same styles into stock. So, I started learning about lean manufacturing. I took out all the work-in-progress (WIP), sold off old stock, created a bonus system, redesigned the factory to improve flow, reduced lead times, and boosted on-time deliveries from 23% to 86%. We split the factory into cells, consolidated most piecework rates into the standard rate, and used key performance indicators to drive improvements. I even replaced the conveyor belt in the sewing area with circular sewing cells so the women could talk to each other—and I added plants to make the place feel nicer.

The company started making money. I felt successful; it was exciting, and I was important.

I bought a converted barn, my daughter got into a good school, and I drove a brand new special edition Racing Green Audi A4.

What could go wrong? I was getting everything I wanted. I was consumed with achieving success and the status that came with it.

But one day, in Pizza Hut at the Metro Centre, my wife told me she'd had enough. I was consumed with work, and she said I had to choose: family or career. I tried to explain that everything I was doing at work was *for* the family. Absolute bollocks. It was for me.

Then came the precipice.

It's May 1998, I'm 36 years old, and it's 10:30 on a Monday morning. I'm standing on a cliff in Tynemouth, wearing a suit and holding a briefcase. The sky is overcast, and there's a brisk wind.

It's about 40–50 feet to the rocks and sea below, and I'm staring into space.

This isn't about suicidal thoughts. It's about knowing that I had truly messed everything up this time.

I had just left the company where I was General Manager. A few weeks earlier, I had told the MD that I wanted out. On this day, an hour earlier, he had called me into his office to tell me they had found my replacement, and he would be starting the next day.

He handed me £7,500 to leave quietly and let me keep my Audi A4 for six months.

I stood up, went to my office, collected my few personal belongings, and walked out the front door, telling the receptionist I was "just popping out."

A year earlier, they had said I was the best operations manager they'd ever had. I had completely overhauled the company's operations, turning it around and making it successful. I thought I was in control of my destiny.

But I wasn't.

Yes, I had asked to leave, but I suspect they had been pushing me out. Why? Maybe they were trying to buy out the owner without him knowing, and they wanted someone who would be a part of that—and that wasn't me. Or maybe I had dropped the ball. My mind was elsewhere.

In February of that same year, I had walked away from a 15-year marriage, moved out of my four-bedroom converted barn, and lost my mistress. I was now living above a hairdresser's in Tynemouth. My daughter stayed with her mother, but we had agreed on shared custody.

It was about as much of a midlife crisis as you could get.

> A MID-LIFE CRISIS IS WHEN YOU WAKE UP WITH EVERYTHING AND YOU ARE STILL UNHAPPY
>
> TOM HANKS

After a while of just standing on that cliff, I walked back onto Tynemouth High Street and returned to my small rented flat above the hairdressers. I sat there, numb.

Tynemouth is a nice place, but on Friday and Saturday nights, it felt like Dodge City in the Old West. From my flat, I'd listen to the sounds of drunken nights—women's laughter, fights, and general revelry. At 2 a.m., the pub next door would dump its empty beer bottles into a skip right under my window just to make sure I was awake. People often told me I should have gone out and joined the fun, but at that time, I could think of nothing worse.

Over the next few months, I focused on finding a new job. I still had a mortgage to pay and child support obligations. Without a computer, I walked to the North Shields library to write letters, send job applications, and look through newspapers for opportunities. (The internet was still in its infancy.)

I felt an overwhelming sense of emptiness—a tremendous hole in my life. To alleviate the sadness and frustration, I walked. Miles every day. When I was still working, but already on my own, I would walk from St. Mary's lighthouse to Tynemouth and back just to shake the feeling of loss. It was about 3 or 4 miles. I remember one Saturday walking around the perimeter of Sainsbury's in Monkseaton twice. Why? I had to.

I was trying to figure out what that emptiness was. Was it losing my job? Partly, yes. So much of my status and self-worth was tied up in work. When it was gone, it wasn't just the money I lost; it was the deference, the feeling of importance. I was the General Manager. People listened to me. Now, I was a nobody.

Was it leaving my wife? Yes, that was part of it too. We had grown apart for some time, and I'd had a few romantic diversions—nothing serious, just the thrill of the chase. The last few months of our marriage, though, I had fallen head over heels for someone else. That made me realise I didn't love my wife anymore, and it was better for both of us to move on. It was selfish, but at the time, I thought it was the right thing to do. Even now, I believe it was the right decision, though I was a poor husband.

The day I left the house, I asked my wife not to let our daughter watch me drive away. But there she stood at the gate, holding our child's hand as I left. It hurt then. It hurts now.

That was part of the emptiness—feeling lost, an aching void.

Was it losing my mistress? Definitely. I loved her. But I never expected her to leave her comfortable life for me. Who would want to be with a broken man? She was beautiful, intelligent, and full of personality. How we got together is still a mystery to me. She soon left me and stayed with her husband. It was a wise decision.

I did the usual things. I went to the doctor, who prescribed anti-depressants. I met with a psychologist to talk through my issues. But none of it really helped. Or if I *did* feel better, I wasn't sure if it was just the drugs.

In the end, it wasn't for me. I stopped taking the pills and thanked the psychologist but declined further sessions.

One person did stand by me, though—a true friend I'd only known for a few months. I haven't seen her in years, but she helped me through some of the darkest days. I think I once made a pass at her, but she declined politely and wisely.

Sometimes, people come into your life unexpectedly, help immensely, and then leave. That's what happened. I hope I can be that kind of friend to someone someday, just as she was to me.

I knew I had gotten myself into this mess, and it was up to me to get out of it.

But how?

I wasn't a bad man (though reading this, you might disagree). I was kind to old people and animals. So why was this happening to me?

I fell in love—so what? Who made the rules that said I couldn't love who I wanted? Who was I to break those rules? What law did I break to be punished like this?

Was it a mental breakdown? Or something else?

One day, I was driving back from a job interview in Glasgow. My thoughts were circling, as usual, until suddenly, I found myself smiling. Then I started laughing. I was going back to nothing. Except for my daughter, everything was gone. I had nothing to laugh about, but the release was immense.

It lasted only a few minutes before the worries crept back in, but the memory of that feeling—the sheer release—has stayed with me.

I'm still not sure what it was.

"

WHEN ILLUSION SPINS HER NET, I REMEMBER WHERE I WANT TO BE, AND LIBERTY, SHE PIROUETTES WHEN I THINK THAT I AM FREE.

SALISBURY HILL, PETER GABRIEL

"

Adventures in Justice, Laws, and Rules

What is justice?

"

JUST CONDUCT; FAIRNESS; EXERCISE OF AUTHORITY IN THE MAINTENANCE OF RIGHT; JUDICIAL PROCEEDINGS.

THE OXFORD ILLUSTRATED DICTIONARY, SECOND EDITION, 1984

"

Do we live in a world of justice and fairness? These qualities seem to be personal, internal attributes, while the exercise of authority—what the police or courts do to us if we break the laws—feels external.

So, which are we: the internal or the external?

We're both. We're a microcosm of the world we live in. The conflicts, loves, and prejudices we experience within ourselves are mirrored in the broader world. The more I think about it, the more obvious it seems.

At any time, we can be fair and just, standing up for what we believe is right. But at other times, we can behave unfairly, with our rights taken away.

Take identity cards as an example of how our perceptions change. Before mobile phones, there was a heated debate about issuing everyone identity cards that could be demanded by authorities. Human rights activists raged against it, calling it an invasion of privacy—1984, Big Brother—and the idea never took off.

Now, we willingly carry mobile phones, which allow authorities to track us at any moment.

The point is, many of us fiercely defend our rights—until it suits us to give them away.

So, what does Socrates, the Greek philosopher, say about justice?

> SOCRATES SEEKS TO DEFINE JUSTICE AS ONE OF THE CARDINAL HUMAN VIRTUES, AND HE UNDERSTANDS THE VIRTUES AS STATES OF THE SOUL. SO HIS ACCOUNT OF WHAT JUSTICE IS DEPENDS UPON HIS ACCOUNT OF THE HUMAN SOUL. ACCORDING TO THE REPUBLIC, EVERY HUMAN SOUL HAS THREE PARTS: REASON, SPIRIT, AND APPETITE.
>
> STANFORD ENCYCLOPEDIA OF PHILOSOPHY, APRIL 1, 2003

In *Plato's Republic,* Thrasymachus, a student of Plato, argued that Socrates' definition of justice was wrong. He claimed:

1. Justice is *"nothing other than the advantage of the stronger."*
2. Justice is obeying the laws of the ruler(s).
3. Justice is *"really someone else's good, the advantage of the man who is stronger and rules."*

Why do we obey the laws of the rulers? Who put them in charge?

Parents, supervisors, managers, judges, politicians—they all try to tell us what to do. Who made them the rulers?

World War I marked a turning point for justice, laws, and rules. In 1901, 1.5 million people were employed in domestic service in Britain, according to the Office for National Statistics. (By 2012, there were still 65,000.) The gap between the haves and have-nots was vast. Up until 1871, you could even buy a commission in the British Army if you had enough money.

Even during World War I, most officers came from the upper or middle classes. The working class knew their place—they followed their "betters" to maintain the social order. And millions died doing just that.

After the war, having fought alongside the upper classes, the working and middle classes saw them for what they were—not better, just richer.

Rules

> “PRINCIPLE TO WHICH ACTION OR PROCEDURE CONFORMS OR IS BOUND OR INTENDED TO CONFORM; DOMINANT CUSTOM, CANON, TEST, STANDARD, NORMAL STATE OF THINGS; USUALLY, MORE OFTEN THAN NOT, IN REGULAR MANNER, MECHANICALLY.
>
> THE OXFORD ILLUSTRATED DICTIONARY, SECOND EDITION, 1984”

> RULES ARE FOR THE OBEDIENCE OF FOOLS AND THE GUIDANCE OF WISE MEN.
>
> HARRY DAY, WWI FIGHTER ACE

There are formal and informal rules. Don't say this or that. Don't upset people (especially with the truth). Don't break the law. Most laws, when you think about it, are there to protect the *haves* from the *have-nots.*

Thrasymachus also argued that if you could get away with it, it would be better to break all the rules for your own benefit. Plato ultimately dismisses this idea of justice as a means for the powerful to stay in power—but he doesn't argue that the current system of justice is right either.

Plato's solution was the *Philosopher King*—a wise ruler who makes decisions based on what's right, not what's popular. People, recognising the king's wisdom, would accept his decisions.

Really? Wouldn't that be great? A wise ruler making all the big decisions while we just live our lives in peace. But would society allow it?

When I was young, there was a craze for amateur radio. People set up antennas to talk anonymously to strangers, sharing news, interests, and views. But soon, it was taken over by people spreading spite and anger. What started as fun became dangerous.

These people were the ancestors of today's online trolls and before them, the people who wrote poison pen letters.

With so many views and opinions swirling around today—from the internet, television, newspapers, and social media—can we ever agree on what justice is?

I believe in freedom of speech. But people should stand behind what they say, not throw anonymous hand grenades just because they can. If you believe in something, put your name to it.

So, was Thrasymachus right? Should we just break the rules to suit ourselves?

I remember once being on duty at the Samaritans with a lovely lady who firmly believed that all young people who broke the law should be birched to teach them a lesson. I asked her if she had ever sped in her car. She admitted that she did, like everyone else. I smiled and asked, *"When should I book you in for a good thrashing, then?"*

Her response was classic: what was "breaking the law" to her was what *others* did. What *she* did was just bending the rules. But, of course, it wasn't.

Anarchy

> A: ABSENCE OF GOVERNMENT.
> B: A STATE OF LAWLESSNESS OR POLITICAL DISORDER DUE TO THE ABSENCE OF GOVERNMENTAL AUTHORITY.
> C: A UTOPIAN SOCIETY OF INDIVIDUALS WHO ENJOY COMPLETE FREEDOM WITHOUT GOVERNMENT.
>
> MERRIAM WEBSTER DICTIONARY

Interesting, isn't it? The definition begins with the *fact* of an absence of government, moves to the *outcome* of lawlessness, and ends with the *dream*—a utopian society.

I'm not advocating for anarchy. I wish for a utopian society, but I don't think that's human nature.

> MAY YOU LIVE IN INTERESTING TIMES
>
> CHINESE CURSE

Once, years ago, I was in church. At the start of the sermon, the vicar played John Lennon's *Imagine*. The song, with its vision of peace and love, filled the room. But after it ended, there was a pause. The vicar, in his dry Yorkshire way, then said, *"Wouldn't that be boring?"*

It's not in man's nature to simply accept things as they are. We're wired to push boundaries. The problem is most of that striving is for more money, prestige, and power—rather than for the good of all.

> "WHEN THE IDEA OF PRIVATE PROPERTY DEVELOPED, SOCIETY HAD TO DEVELOP A SYSTEM TO PROTECT IT. THIS SYSTEM EVOLVED AS LAWS IMPOSED BY THOSE WITH PROPERTY ONTO THOSE WITHOUT PROPERTY.
>
> JEAN-JACQUES ROUSSEAU, THE SOCIAL CONTRACT (1762)"

(Karl Marx was heavily influenced by Rousseau—not Groucho, though, that would've been something.)

If the universe is, as I believe, a microcosm of ourselves, then change has to start with the self. If you want to change the world, change yourself.

> THOU HYPOCRITE, FIRST CAST OUT THE BEAM OUT OF THINE OWN EYE; AND THEN SHALT THOU SEE CLEARLY TO CAST OUT THE MOTE OUT OF THY BROTHER'S EYE.
>
> THE NEW TESTAMENT, MATTHEW 7:5

Let's put our own house in order first.

Philo = the love of
Sophy = wisdom
Wis = wise
Dom (or doom) = decisions

How do we make wise decisions when we're surrounded by conflicting views? Here's a simple framework (I can't claim credit for this—probably borrowed it from the School of Philosophy):

1. Is my decision good for me?
2. Is my decision good for my family?
3. Is my decision good for my country? (*Yorkshire, obviously.*)
4. Is my decision good for society?

If the answer to all of these is *yes*, then you're probably on the right track.

Justice, Laws, and Rules

So, how do we achieve justice and establish our own rules?

By continuing to learn and applying that knowledge—knowledge born of experience—with the love of wisdom. That's how we begin to create our own rules and justice. If everyone did the same, society would evolve.

Until then, I view justice, laws, and rules as necessary. They're imperfect, sure, but they're better than nothing, and they've stood the test of time. Still, that doesn't mean we stop questioning them. We should always be thinking and always awake to how things can be improved.

"

RENDER UNTO CAESAR THE THINGS THAT ARE CAESAR'S, AND UNTO GOD THE THINGS THAT ARE GOD'S.

THE NEW TESTAMENT,

MATTHEW 22:15

"

(Swap "God" for whatever you like—consciousness, spirit, the self, or nothing at all.)

Personal Justice

So, did I deserve the loneliness and pain I suffered during that time? Was it justice? Probably.

I had broken the wedding vows I had taken willingly. I had pursued my own selfish desires—both in love and in my quest for success. And I had hurt people along the way.

CHAPTER EIGHT

THE LOST YEARS

Eventually, after a few months, I found another job with Freudenberg in Greetland, near Halifax, and I left the Northeast and returned to Yorkshire. It wasn't planned, but the pull of Yorkshire, the offer of a job and the chance to run away from my failures and hide seemed like a good idea at the time.

The new job paid two-thirds of what I earned in the North East, working in nonwoven sales. Sales? I had had enough of Operations, I wanted something different. At first, I drove down on Monday mornings, stayed at cheap B&Bs during the week, and drove back to the flat on Friday evenings.

My wife and I got divorced—unreasonable behaviour, apparently. I didn't disagree. I didn't have a solicitor; just accepted what her solicitor suggested. We split the money: two-thirds to her and our child, and one-third to me. I paid the costs. I wasn't a good husband, and I knew it.

Eventually, I rented a small house in Brighouse from a hairdresser who had moved in with her boyfriend. The Audi had to go back. So, I bought an old Nissan. I still walked miles every day trying to walk off the mental pain. Old mates and family kept in touch, which helped but I still had that feeling of emptiness. Three out of four Saturdays were spent driving up to Newcastle to see my daughter. Any spare money went on petrol and entertaining her from 9:45 a.m. to 5 p.m. It always started with breakfast at McDonald's at the Silverlink, then a trip to the cinema, followed by Pizza Hut and a walk around Tynemouth or a castle.

I kept going; the ex-wife was sometimes helpful, but other times, she slammed the door in my face. Potluck, really.

In December of that year, I moved into a house near where I worked. I'm still in it. I had no furniture, just a bed and a few wicker chairs. I bought a new suite and took a TV from the old house. The place needed decorating, but I had no money to do it. It had been rented out before I bought it, and the previous tenants had hung pictures of six-inch nails on the wall.

That Christmas, I spent alone in my new house. I bought a fake Christmas tree and hung some leftover decorations from my old place. One night, I heard a noise and saw a mouse trying to pull one of the chocolate baubles off the tree. Grim. I got invites from family for Christmas dinner, but I couldn't face it. Yes, it was bad. I did go up to Newcastle the next day and brought my daughter down, so it was just one day on my own. Still, it felt bad.

> ISN'T IT FUNNY THAT AT CHRISTMAS SOMETHING IN YOU GETS SO LONELY FOR I DON'T KNOW WHAT EXACTLY, BUT IT'S SOMETHING THAT YOU DON'T MIND NOT HAVING AT OTHER TIMES.
>
> KATE L BOSHER (1865–1932)

I joined a dating company for professionals. They set up an interview with me, and my profile was sent out. It cost a bomb—way more than the online stuff now, but I needed to fill that emptiness. I met one woman, recently divorced, who turned up in a fur coat. She probably thought "professional" meant "rich," which I certainly wasn't. That only lasted one dinner.

I met another woman in York, she was lovely—but that night, I got a taste for beer, and we ended up doing a pub crawl. I had a great time, but I don't think she did. That was that. Then there was a dentist I saw a few times, but she wasn't my type. Does desperation have a type?

She complained that I hadn't tried it on with her. Apparently, her friend from the same dating club was getting shagged nearly every night by different blokes.

Then it hit me—I wasn't getting anywhere with these women because I wasn't shagging them. I was looking for romance and a spark; they were just after a quick shag. I left the agency. Why did I do that? What was wrong with me?

I had a dalliance with a woman from work. She was young and pretty. We sent dirty emails to each other until she had a day off, and one of her colleagues opened her inbox—she nearly had a heart attack. I can be very descriptive. She reported us both, and we both got a final written warning. The promotion that was on the cards got cancelled.

Sometimes, I wish I was making this up. I really do.

I had only been with the company for a short period of time, but I had already messed up.

It was time to leave the world of sales. I'd done alright and increased my sales figures, but I kept drifting back into production whenever customers complained about poor quality. I'd go in, trying to fix things, with some success. Then, senior operations management asked me—a salesman—to redesign their warehouse. After a year and a quarter, I found myself heading back into operations.

At this point, I'd been on my own for nearly two years.

- The first year, I hated it.
- The second year, I got used to it.
- The third year, I started to enjoy it.

One weekend, early in my lost years, a female friend from Newcastle came down to Halifax to join me at a company. That weekend, we visited Haworth and checked out the New World shop. They had a Tarot card reading service.

I don't believe in that sort of thing, but the man who read my cards said I'd gone through dramatic change and wouldn't find true love for three years.

I don't believe in it, but he got it spot on.

Was that my sentence? Three years of being alone as punishment for the upset I'd caused in the Northeast. Tarot cards can't be real, can they? They cannot tell the truth.

Adventures in Truth

What is truth? How can it be found, and what are its benefits?

truth
noun /tru:θ/

> THE TRUE FACTS ABOUT SOMETHING, RATHER THAN THINGS THAT HAVE BEEN INVENTED OR GUESSED.
>
> (SOURCE: OXFORD ADVANCED LEARNER'S DICTIONARY)

Can truth ever change? A cut flower is beautiful now, but in a few weeks' time, it'll be dry and falling to bits. Is it still beautiful?

What about facts? Can they change? No, but are they always what they seem?

It's difficult to separate fact from fiction, truth from lies.

> I THINK, THEREFORE I AM.
>
> RENÉ DESCARTES,
> MEDITATIONS ON FIRST PHILOSOPHY
> (1640)

I used to laugh at this quote. By the same logic, I'd joke, that if you quack, you must be a duck.

But I was wrong. It's a profound statement. The only thing you can truly be sure of is that if you're thinking, you exist. It's solid, even if your thoughts are crazy or stupid—the fact that you're thinking means you exist. That's the truth. From there, it gets a lot trickier.

How do you know what's true?

I visited the Newark Civil War Museum recently, and on the top floor was an exhibition on false news. It highlighted how, during the English Civil War, both sides produced propaganda, each accusing the other of atrocities. Some of it was true, but a lot wasn't. And this was the 17th century.

There were also two photographs of U.S. presidential inaugurations—one of Barack Obama's and the other of Donald Trump's. The first picture showed a packed crowd outside the White House for Obama. The second showed a half-full crowd (being generous) for Trump. TV news reported there were more people at Obama's inauguration, backed by official numbers.

Donald Trump said this wasn't true and claimed more people attended his ceremony. It was obviously not true. His staff started calling these statements "alternative facts." In Yorkshire, we call it lying.

With so many "truths" out there, how can we know what's true? Our "truth" is based on our opinions, and those opinions are shaped by our upbringing—our parents, social status, friends, teachers, and even the news we watch.

Nowadays, companies analyse your spending habits and online activity to figure out your opinions, likes, and dislikes. Then they send you information, publicity, and articles confirming you're right in your views (who would have guessed that?), all to sell you something—or to get your vote.

Distorting the truth has become an art form.

A LIE TOLD OFTEN ENOUGH BECOMES THE TRUTH.

VLADIMIR LENIN

Can we get to the truth? Let's go back to Descartes:

I AM HERE QUITE ALONE, AND AT LAST I WILL DEVOTE MYSELF SINCERELY AND WITHOUT RESERVATION TO THE GENERAL DEMOLITION OF MY OPINIONS.

RENÉ DESCARTES,
MEDITATIONS ON FIRST PHILOSOPHY (1640)

I really like this. Descartes fully accepts that his opinions—his truths—are potentially wrong, and he sets out to demolish them to see things as they truly are. In doing so, he frees himself from all the false, circulating thoughts, wearisome worries, and damaging prejudices.

> “PREJUDICE IS A GREAT TIMESAVER. YOU CAN FORM OPINIONS WITHOUT HAVING TO GET THE FACTS.
>
> E.B. WHITE”

I've met many people in my life of different religions, races, and colours. Some have been wonderful; some have been right dicks. But it never seemed like their race, religion, or colour had anything to do with it. If you're a dick, you're a dick.

I've always voted Labour. My mother and father voted Labour, and I'm working class. However, I got as close to not voting Labour as I ever have at the last election, when Corbyn was leader. I really had to think about it. I disliked his policies almost as much as I disliked the Tories. Or was it just prejudice? I don't like Tories—that's a prejudice.

Prejudice wastes time and energy. I often joke about how much I dislike that team based in Salford. All my prejudices are neatly packed against that football team. But I know it's nonsense. Once we understand the world, we can play, have a laugh, and tease—it's part of life. I never forget, though, that it's all nonsense. I only tease those I know will take it the right way. I never joke about racism, ageism, or someone's religion.

People often feel offended by personal slights. In contrast, I find poverty, greed, and prejudice deeply offensive. However, life is meant to be enjoyed, and philosophy should guide us toward a joyful existence.

The issue with Descartes' attempt to destroy his opinions is this: What's left after you've done that?

And that's where his famous line— "I think, therefore I am"—comes in.

If you're thinking, you must exist. That's a truth.

We know one truth: We exist.

It can only be that *we* exist. Someone else thinking doesn't prove they exist.

So, we have a starting point.

Defending Your Truth

In business, I've often come up against people who refuse to change their minds, even when the facts say otherwise. They end up looking foolish, defending the indefensible. Of course, it's all ego. It's even worse when they're the boss.

Defend your point of view until proven wrong, but then accept it. Don't let ego stop you from making progress.

> DOUBT IS NOT A PLEASANT CONDITION, BUT CERTAINTY IS ABSURD.
>
> VOLTAIRE (1694–1778)

I would slightly disagree with Voltaire. We know we exist—that, for me, is a certainty. The rest is difficult to prove, so we have doubts about what's true and what's not.

Where do we go from here?

It comes back to us again.

Firstly, don't give in. There are many people in this world who want you to stop looking for the truth. They don't have to prove their truth is right; they just need to convince you that truth doesn't exist.

"All politicians are liars."

"If voting changed anything, it would be banned."

Are all politicians liars?

Is voting pointless?

Certainly, some just want power, but are they all like that?

Do we just accept that it's not worth trying?

Look at how many people actually vote next time. Those who think nothing will change don't vote, so nothing does change. Heaven forbids they actually try to find the truth. Sounds like waking up.

So, have the people trying to stop you thinking won, or have you lost?

What does Shri Shantananda Saraswati say about truth in the 10 principles of Sanatan Dharma?

PRINCIPLE NINE

“

THE TRUTH. THERE IS ONLY ONE TRUTH ABOUT ANYTHING; THERE CAN'T BE TWO DIFFERENT TRUTHS ABOUT THE SAME SUBJECT. EVERYBODY IN THE WORLD IS HANKERING FOR TRUTH, BUT IT HAPPENS THAT PEOPLE WANT THEIR PARTICULAR BRAND OF TRUTH; THEY ARE NOT EAGER OR READY TO ACCEPT THAT THERE CAN BE SOMETHING DIFFERENT. ONE MAY BE RIGHT OR WRONG, AND THEN RATIONALISATION IS NECESSARY. EVEN THIEVES, ROBBERS, AND EVIL MEN WISH THAT THOSE WITH WHOM THEY COOPERATE SHOULD SPEAK THE TRUTH, SO THEY DON'T GET CAUGHT BY THE POLICE! SO, TRUTH IS IMPORTANT NOT ONLY FOR PEOPLE IN HIGHLY DEVELOPED AND CULTURED SOCIETY; THE NEED IS EVERYWHERE. BUT SOMEHOW, PEOPLE LIKE TO SERVE THEIR OWN ENDS THROUGH THEIR OWN CONCEPT OF TRUTH.

SHRI SHANTANANDA SARASWATI

”

Shri Shantananda gets it right again. Even bad people need some truth.

It's a bit like what the devil says to Jesus on top of the mountain. You don't have to believe in the devil—you just have to not believe in God, and he's won.

Similarly, you don't have to believe in lies; you just have to believe there's no truth.

Summing Up on Truth

There are truths out there. They're hard to find, and there are people actively trying to stop you from finding them. They're trying to take your choice and life away.

“

BUT WE MUSTN'T LET HIM HAVE IT.

GOLLUM, THE LORD OF THE RINGS, J.R.R. TOLKIEN

”

Never give in. Wake up. Enjoy the process.

CHAPTER NINE

BACK TO TEXTILES AND THE MILL

I joined John Holdsworth in Halifax as the Weaving Manager. They made transport fabric for buses, London Underground trains, and coaches.

The Chairlady was Mrs. Holdsworth, and the Managing Director was her son, Michael Holdsworth. His younger brother was the Operations Director, and their sister was the HR Director. The only non-Holdsworth on the board was the Finance Director, who had been with the company for many years.

I was still living on my own, no girlfriend, but beginning to come out of my stupor.

This was an old-fashioned textile mill, but Michael had such enthusiasm for the company (founded by his great-grandfather, I think) that it had a full-order book. Michael was a great salesman—he travelled the world selling the company's product, and he did a good job. He and I became friends.

His brother was different. He said he went to school at Harrow and joked that it made him "Harrogant."

Apparently, this is a Harrow joke. It wasn't funny to me because, well, he *was* arrogant.

They had a paternalistic approach to their employees. Many of the workers were of Asian descent and didn't see it as paternalism—they thought the owners were racist. The employees took liberties with how they worked, clocking each other out and going to the fish and chip shop whenever they pleased. The weavers had dens behind the looms where they'd eat or chat out of sight of management. Discipline was non-existent.

The mill spanned several large Victorian buildings and consisted of Spinning, Weaving, and Finishing, plus the offices. I was the manager of the largest area: Weaving. It was typical of a family business, but a little chaotic. The previous Weaving Manager had been put in charge of Finishing and wasn't too happy about it. Meanwhile, a Holdsworth family friend, another public schoolboy, ran Spinning.

The supervisors were called tuners. There was a day shift and a night shift manager. Everyone had nicknames. The Operations Director was called "Herr Flick" because he looked and acted like the character from *'Allo 'Allo!* The day shift manager was called "Twins" because he had twins, and the night shift manager was "Bulb Head" because he had a bald head. I was called the "Fat Controller" for obvious reasons.

The previous manager was well in with the day shift weaving supervisor, and together, they tried to make my life miserable—unhappy about the implied criticism behind his demotion. On my first day, Twins took me to an office and showed me where to sit —outside his office, with the planner and head tuner.

I don't think so.

I immediately told him his office was now mine, and I moved him to the spot he had planned for me. I promptly had my new office repainted, got a new table, and new lighting—the works.

They started a whispering campaign against me with the other staff and the Director. After about a month, in the Director's office, when Herr Flick asked me how things were going, I smiled at the previous manager and Twins and said.", "I just want to thank these two gentlemen for the support and warm welcome they've given me."

They knew I was lying, but my smile made it clear they couldn't intimidate me.

I'd been shafted by experts before—these guys were no match.

"

IT'S ALWAYS THE GUY WHO'S WILLING TO DIE WHO'S GOING TO WIN THE FIGHT.

AL PACINO, ANY GIVEN SUNDAY

"

Twins became, and still is, a friend.

I had nothing to lose. I didn't fear losing my job or my house. I was still paying maintenance for my daughter, but that was my only real responsibility.

Around this time, I started going to a Tuesday night New Age group meeting in Sowerby Bridge. Some of the talks were alright, but it was mostly "The Power of Crystals" or "Angels on My Shoulder" stuff—not my scene. Still, there were a few women attending, so I kept going. One night, a girl named Siobhan stood up and talked about a philosophy group in Huddersfield. It piqued my interest for two reasons: first, I'd always been interested in philosophy; second, Siobhan was fit.

I joined the course, and three weeks later, I was hooked. It was like turning on a light bulb. Instead of always looking outward for answers, I started looking inward. Siobhan left the group after a few weeks, and I left twenty years later. The initial classes focused on "The Exercise," a method for quieting the mind. I'd need that in the years to come.

The weaving shed worked from 8 a.m. to 4:30 p.m. Monday to Friday and 8 p.m. to 8 a.m. Monday to Thursday. We needed more capacity. Overtime was expensive and relied on the mostly Asian weavers agreeing to do it, which they did when it suited them. We had three banks of six looms, with one weaver managing two looms.

Time for a change.

I worked with the internal and external union officials on a plan to have one weaver manage three looms, with 6-2 and 2-10 rotating shifts, plus a permanent 10-6 shift. The looms took a few hours to change over, so most of the time, weavers were still only responsible for two looms. I increased their hourly rate, got rid of the piece-rate bonus (which caused poor quality), and replaced it with a bonus based on "right first time." We ran an eight-week trial.

It worked. Everyone seemed happy. But to make the change permanent, we needed the weavers to vote to change their contracts. The external union rep oversaw the vote.

The weavers said no.

They wanted more money. The external rep was shocked—there'd been no indication this was going to happen.

There were about 25–30 Asian weavers and 5 white weavers.

What now?

Michael was abroad on business, Herr Flick was nowhere to be seen and wanted to stay out of it, and the HR Director didn't want to get involved. The feeling I got from them was that they didn't want to be associated with failure when it was all my idea.

I remember going home that night to an empty house, feeling pretty miserable. My grand plan had failed. Everyone saw me as either a failure or someone who'd crack under the pressure.

But as I lay in bed, a thought occurred to me:

Fuck it.

Right.

No point in discussing this with the directors—the only one who counted was abroad for six weeks. I'd do it myself.

I kept all the tuners on the new shift pattern, which they preferred. I found out that few white weavers had voted for the change, so I kept one bank of looms on the new shifts with the white weavers. Everyone else went back to their old shifts with no overtime.

Production dropped slightly, but I gave all the available resources to the new shifts.

I generally had a good relationship with the internal and external union reps. The internal rep was a good guy who represented his members well at disciplinary meetings, though the decision almost always went against them. I picked my battles well, and then he'd call in the external rep, and we would end up in the industrial tribunal. Six times we went—I won five. The only case I lost was when the judge asked Michael why he hadn't carried out a full appeal, and his answer was, "If David said he should go, that was good enough for me."

Now, the rep was a bit cocky. With the backing of his weavers, he thought he had me over a barrel. He smiled as if to say, "What can I do? I'm just representing the weavers."

But who would break first?

I made sure to walk the weaving department floor 3-4 times a day. Smiling. Encouraging those who supported the change but still being friendly and confident with those who voted against it. In the first few weeks, they greeted me with knowing smiles because they knew I couldn't force them to sign—I needed the production.

But who would break first?

After a few weeks, slowly, the weavers and then the rep started asking when the next discussions would be.

"There are no next discussions," I said. "There's nothing else to say."

Eight weeks passed. Production was keeping up with sales. The weavers were losing money because I had cut the overtime. Eventually, the rep came to see me. The weavers were ready to accept the new contract if we gave them half of the extra money they'd asked for.

No.

Increased bonus?

No.

Longer breaks?

No.

Another week passed.

Then the rep. said the weavers were willing to take another vote.

"Fine," I said.

They voted and accepted.

There were some toilets underneath my office. One day, while sitting on the toilet, I noticed someone had written on the wall, "Midgeley is a bastard." I crossed it out and wrote, "It's spelt Midgley," and initialled it.

I took a week's holiday to Provence with a group of strangers, all single, to recover. It was an eye-opener in many ways.

The age range was from 30 to 60, with roughly equal numbers of men and women. A few, like me, went for a walking holiday and didn't feel the need to socialise, while others were keen to meet the opposite sex. I think there were around 30 people, and some began relationships within the first 48 hours. I remember two sixty-year-olds starting the first day they met. One or two had multiple partners during the week—no point wasting time, was there? Some, like me, didn't. I wasn't ready.

One night, after a few drinks—alright, a lot of drinks—a girl from London said, "You're so funny," and pulled me into her bedroom.

"Have you got a condom?" she asked.

"No," I said, relieved.

"Oh… well, be careful," she replied, promptly taking off her knickers, lifting her skirt, and lying on the bed.

I looked at her. She was nice, just lonely, like me. But I couldn't do it. It felt wrong. I didn't fancy her. I said sorry and walked out. The next day, I tried to apologise again, but she ignored me for the rest of the week. Is there something wrong with me?

I did fancy a woman from Sutton Coldfield. She was a year older, just coming out of a relationship, and I tried too hard to impress her—ended up scaring her off. Once, we were having a group meal in Avignon when she got up to walk around the town. I asked if she wanted company. She said no. I was devastated.

Another romantic failure. Back to work.

Then, I had to deal with the tuners. Some of them had become a law unto themselves. One was a good tuner but was stealing from the other workers and treating them with contempt.

Eventually, we found evidence of his theft, and I started disciplinary proceedings. It was tough. He couldn't argue with the evidence, but he refused to believe we would dismiss him. He'd built up this aura of invincibility in the mill. People feared him. They didn't think we'd follow through. The other tuners were nervous.

The union couldn't support him because the evidence was too strong.

I dismissed him, and he appealed to the Production Director—Herr Flick.

The tuner came back with a long list of misdemeanours committed by the other tuners, basically throwing them under the bus to save himself.

All the allegations were investigated, but there was no evidence—it was his word against theirs. Though I suspected some of it was true affairs, going home during shifts, that sort of thing.

His wife came in to plead his case, but I had to convince the Operations Director to uphold the decision. To his credit, after about three months, he did.

That night, the tuner went to his local bar and complained to anyone who'd listen about "that bastard David Midgley." He was barred immediately.

The landlady was my sister.

As the news of his dismissal spread, employees—mostly the Asians—came up to shake my hand and thank me. The other tuners stopped any further misbehaviour and were relieved they hadn't been pulled into the investigation.

I felt numb. It was hard. Once again, it felt like I was taking on the world by myself.

Over the first couple of years, I dismissed up to thirty people for various reasons.

There were the two lads who worked nights and always got a "migraine" at 2 a.m. on Thursdays. They'd go home for a couple of hours' sleep, then start at 8 a.m. at a local garage for the weekend.

Then there were the creelers who were absent one or two days a week—no shoes to wear, or they were "ill" (usually from drinking).

There was fighting in the canteen area. Once, it was between an old creeler and a young assistant weaver, both Asian. I brought them into my office and gave them both a written warning. That night, the old creeler visited the younger one, and with the lad's father, they beat him up. We never saw him again.

Some people who were off sick were working somewhere else to see if they preferred to work at Holdsworth's.

Others were nipping out for fish and chips for themselves and their mates.

And, of course, clocking each other out when they had gone home early.

My favourite issue wasn't a dismissal, but when the warping team came to me and said they could re-warp four looms a day, not the usual three if I paid them more money. I politely declined but told them I'd reduce their wages by a quarter because they could already do the three looms in fewer hours.

This was the legacy of years of bad management.

I was the new sheriff, cleaning up the town.

Over the next couple of years, productivity and quality improved, but the company was under pressure to cut costs due to competition from companies subsidised by their governments. Redundancies were necessary to keep the company solvent. I hated making people redundant. I once saw a picture of Stalin signing death sentences, and I looked very similar—redundancy letters on one side, final settlements on the other, and a box of tissues for those who needed it. Usually, it was me.

I could handle those who shouted and swore at me, but it was the ones who showed dignity and empathy that hurt the most. I stuck to the principle of being hard-nosed about the act itself. Saying you'll "take another look" because someone's crying and wondering how they're going to pay their mortgage only helps *you*, not them. It just prolongs their agony.

The unions took the company to court over some individuals, but they always lost. You have to choose between person A or person B, and as long as you could show that you were being as fair as possible, you were fine. I really tried to be fair—for my own conscience, not for the company's.

Michael ended up dismissing his friend in Spinning and asked me to take over all the manufacturing departments. The Operations Director began writing a history of the company. He was very excited one day when he showed me he'd managed to get a picture of smoke coming out of the mill chimney on the website. Well, I could not do that!

So, when you've dismissed people, forced contract changes, and made redundancies, how do you lift the staff and move forward? Training.

I worked with the Huddersfield Textile Centre of Excellence, secured some funding, and started a training programme. NVQ2/3's for the shop floor, NEBSS, and DMS for the staff. The trainers were excellent. Some of the Asians had very poor English, but with the support of the trainers, they achieved certificates—often the only qualifications they'd ever received. I think we trained up to a hundred people.

Morale on the shop floor was good. There was discipline. If you did a good job, you were told so. If you took the piss, you were dealt with.

Nothing brings down morale like good people watching bad people get away with murder. It's tough for management, but necessary to maintain and improve morale.

I also began more training myself. I had a technical degree in textiles, but now I enrolled at Huddersfield University to get an MBA. Another three long years. The course was initially paid for by Holdsworth's and then by the next company I worked for. I consider myself very fortunate to have had that support.

Where did I find the confidence to fight the union and make difficult decisions with no backup from senior management, no home life, no love life, and no financial safety net?

All I had was a desire to do what was right. Fear is the mind-killer. I had nothing to lose. It had all gone. I was free.

Adventures in Freedom

What is freedom? Freedom, to me, is the biggest reason I started exploring philosophy.

The Inuit apparently have over 40 words for snow. I think there could be 40 definitions of freedom.

The *Oxford Illustrated Dictionary*, second edition (1984), defines freedom as:

freedom
noun /ˈfriːdəm/

Personal liberty; exemption or release from slavery or imprisonment; civil liberty, independence; liberty of action; power of self-determination; independence of fate or necessity.

I'm lucky enough to live in a society where I don't need to fight against tyranny or slavery. Although I disagree with many of my country's decisions in recent years, it's a democracy. I can write this. I have, generally, political freedom, even if not always societal freedom.

At that time, I had freedom from responsibility. This gave me a sense of release, especially in monetary terms. I still paid child maintenance, and I had a mortgage, but I knew I could get a job—even if not a great one—if things went south. I'd been through major trauma, and I knew I'd survive. I had no one to answer to.

Sounds great, right? But I was lonely and full of self-doubt. I tried chatting up a woman from work, but she kindly declined. It left me feeling hollow, especially when word spread around the mill. I had some hope, but of what? Picking back up the responsibilities I'd only just put down?

Circling thoughts, sleepless nights, no direction—it was difficult to see a way forward.

What about internal freedom? Freedom from negative thoughts?

“

THERE IS ONLY ONE DECISION YOU NEED TO MAKE: YOU ARE EITHER WORKING AT YOUR FREEDOM, OR YOU ARE ACCEPTING YOUR BONDAGE.

ROBERT ADAMS

”

They say the first step to facing a problem is realising that it exists. I had to break away from the circling thoughts and start seeing myself clearly. This is where the School of Philosophy—the group I'd joined in Huddersfield—really helped.

Slowly, over time, I began to get control over my thoughts.

The realisation that your thoughts are separate from who you truly are and can be misleading, was a powerful one. To see your thoughts as an observer was quite scary at first. Who is doing the thinking, and who is doing the observing?

Sometimes, you don't even realise you're in bondage until you begin to see the chains.

"

MINDFULNESS GIVES YOU TIME. TIME GIVES YOU CHOICES. CHOICES, SKILLFULLY MADE, LEAD TO FREEDOM. YOU DON'T HAVE TO BE SWEPT AWAY BY YOUR FEELINGS. YOU CAN RESPOND WITH WISDOM AND KINDNESS RATHER THAN HABIT AND REACTIVITY.

HENEPOLA GUNARATANA

"

If this realisation is true, then why isn't everyone searching for freedom?

"

MOST PEOPLE DO NOT REALLY WANT FREEDOM, BECAUSE FREEDOM INVOLVES RESPONSIBILITY, AND MOST PEOPLE ARE FRIGHTENED OF RESPONSIBILITY.

SIGMUND FREUD

"

Here we go, back to *Waking Sleep*. People generally don't want to wake up. Maybe some are naturally awake, while others choose to stay asleep (I think everyone has their moments).

Once you're free and awake, you become truly responsible for your actions as an individual—and that can be uncomfortable. There's no more excuse.

"

CONFORMITY IS THE JAILER OF FREEDOM AND THE ENEMY OF GROWTH.

JOHN F. KENNEDY

"

How much time do we spend trying to fit in? Is it wrong to fit in? There's safety in conformity—no need to rock the boat. You might as well stay asleep.

"

IT IS DIFFICULT TO FREE FOOLS FROM THE CHAINS THEY REVERE.

VOLTAIRE

"

If you're happy with your chains, keep them and be happy—especially if you're aware of them and can live with them. My concern is with those people who feel frustrated and angry because of the chains they cling to and don't want to lose.

To capture monkeys in the forest, sometimes they put a container in the ground with sweets or food inside. The monkeys can just barely get their hands in to grab the sweets, but they can't pull their hands out while holding the food. They won't let go of the sweets, so they're trapped and captured.

If you're happy being asleep, stop reading and be happy.

I wasn't.

> TRUE FREEDOM IS ALWAYS SPIRITUAL. IT HAS SOMETHING TO DO WITH YOUR INNERMOST BEING, WHICH CANNOT BE CHAINED, HANDCUFFED, OR PUT INTO A JAIL.
>
> RAJNEESH

This is true, but only if you need spiritual freedom. If you don't need it, if you're content, then it's not for me or anyone else to tell you to do anything different.

I followed my path out of necessity. I had no choice, really. I was unhappy and searching for a solution. It might not be your path.

There's something I've mentioned before: teaching a pig to dance.

It's a waste of time—and it annoys the pig.

It's the same with trying to teach people about consciousness and freedom. If they're not interested, it's a waste of time and only annoys them.

> “AT THIS TIME IS FREEDOM ANYTHING BUT THE RIGHT TO LIVE AS WE WISH? NOTHING ELSE.
>
> EPICTETUS”

Freedom is different for everyone. For me, it was about gaining control over my emotions—something I still struggle with, but at least now I know what I'm struggling against.

> I HAVE WALKED THAT LONG ROAD TO FREEDOM. I HAVE TRIED NOT TO FALTER; I HAVE MADE MISSTEPS ALONG THE WAY. BUT I HAVE DISCOVERED THE SECRET THAT AFTER CLIMBING A GREAT HILL, ONE ONLY FINDS THAT THERE ARE MANY MORE HILLS TO CLIMB. I HAVE TAKEN A MOMENT HERE TO REST, TO STEAL A VIEW OF THE GLORIOUS VISTA THAT SURROUNDS ME, TO LOOK BACK ON THE DISTANCE I HAVE COME. BUT I CAN ONLY REST FOR A MOMENT, FOR WITH FREEDOM COMES RESPONSIBILITIES, AND I DARE NOT LINGER, FOR MY LONG WALK IS NOT ENDED.
>
> NELSON MANDELA

It's not an easy journey, and it never ends. As Nelson Mandela says, you may falter, but you must keep going.

The School of Philosophy – The Early Years

Since this is something I was involved in for twenty years, and it's a theme I'll return to throughout the book, the school needs some explanation.

The philosophical group I joined in Huddersfield was part of an organisation called *The School of Philosophy*. They also go by the name *The School of Economic Science*, which I think sounds dreadful.

The School of Philosophy is a teaching charity based in London. It was founded in the 1930s by a man named

Leon McLaren following the Great Depression. It began by exploring the economic reasons behind the stock market crash but later shifted towards philosophical understanding. They still offer economics classes.

The school teaches that philosophy isn't just a belief system—it's a way of life. In the early terms, the school covers a wide range of philosophies, but over time, the focus shifts to Advaita philosophy. This is an ancient Indian philosophy, meaning "Not Two," popularised by Shri Shantananda Saraswati, the Shankaracharya of Northern India, during the 1950s–70s. However, the philosophy itself dates back thousands of years.

The school has been called a cult, and there was even a book titled *The Secret Cult,* written by two journalists from the *London Evening Standard.* I read it early in my journey with the school, and while much of it was true, it was heavily sensationalised. They made a big deal about judges, lawyers, and other establishment figures being members, which was true at one time. I don't know if that's still the case.

If you're part of a school or society that explores the spiritual side of life, people tend to call it a cult. The irony is that *The Secret Cult* knew all about the school's teachings and activities—so not much of a secret then.

If it is a cult, it's the worst cult ever.

There are no drugs, no sex, no guns, no money, and you can leave whenever you like.

I'm not here to promote the school. It helped me, but I've since left for reasons I'll explain later. The first few terms, though, are great at wakening up if you want to wake up—if that's what you're after.

Glaive was my first tutor, and he's still a friend today. Patient, kind, and understanding, he's now in his seventies and still teaches.

The school follows a Socratic method, where the tutor reads out philosophical texts, and the group—arranged in a semi-circle—discusses them.

They also give you tools you can use in everyday life. A kind of toolkit.

In those first few weeks, the School of Philosophy started to teach me.

The Exercise

Focusing on the body and breathing for a few minutes in the morning and evening helped to quiet the mind.

Pausing

Between actions, take a moment to allow time to finish one task before starting the next to prevent life from becoming one giant marathon of doing.

What Would a Wise Man Do?

In any situation, pause to avoid reacting automatically the way you always have. Think to yourself, what would a wise man do?

Not This, Not This

Whatever you're thinking, remember—you are not that.

Treat People as if for the First Time

Put aside preconceptions and see people, even those you don't like, as if for the first time.

I would recommend the first three years at the School of Philosophy to anyone. My quest for newfound freedom kept me at the School in Huddersfield for two terms, but the class diminished to the point where it wasn't viable anymore. This was mainly due to a philosophical debate that erupted one night.

The topic was, "Why do we perform our actions—out of love or out of fear?" It came out of nowhere and it was certainly not the intention and wasn't something Glaive had planned, but it escalated into a major row within the group.

Do you go to work because you love it, or because you fear losing your house or family if you don't?

Do you visit your parents out of love, or out of duty or fear of the repercussions of not seeing them?

Do you exercise because you love it, or because you fear getting ill if you don't?

Do you get married because you love the person, or because you fear society's judgment if you don't?

Do you live your life in love or fear? This question applies to any action you take. Sometimes, it may be love, sometimes fear.

It's a good question. But some in the group want to face it. I think a few of them began waking up.

Half the group left that week. I enjoyed the debate, but I came to the uncomfortable conclusion that many of my actions were motivated by fear. I didn't like that realisation. The class became too small to continue.

I was told I could join another class at the same level in the bigger Leeds branch; the school owned its own building and was the centre for the Northeast. So off to Leeds, I went, and I stopped attending the New Age group in Sowerby Bridge.

On my first night in Leeds, I met two women, both named Janet. They were friends and had been in the school for the same amount of time as me. They'd come to the school as yoga teachers which shares many of the same philosophies. I sat next to one of the Janets, who talked freely with me. The other Janet hardly spoke at all. There was also an IT expert and a few other attendees, mostly white, upper-working-class or middle-class.

The school gave me a sense that there might be answers to the questions I had.

After a few terms, you were expected to give "service". All the tutors were also students and volunteered their time, so you were expected to do the same.

Service basically meant giving up time to help with other groups. I started going back to Huddersfield to serve tea, sell philosophical books, or help with group administration. No one was paid—it was all run by volunteers. If you were serving tea, you were expected to bake cakes or biscuits to sell (any money went to pay for the room rentals).

I went to the Supermarket and bought Jaffa Cakes and doughnuts instead. This was great because any leftovers were mine to eat. I'm not stupid.

I was still competitive; Huddersfield sold more books than any other branch because I flirted with all the women to get them to buy books. Well, it was better than carrying them around and laying them out each night.

These early terms at the school helped me cope with all the other stresses in my life. The two Janets in Leeds became friends, especially the quiet one. We started talking on the phone outside of classes.

One night in class, I received a message saying that my mother, who had been living in a care home, was seriously ill, and I needed to get to the Bradford Royal Infirmary as soon as possible.

I drove straight to the hospital and went to the ward. A nurse approached me and asked what I wanted. I told her I had come to see my mother, Jean Midgley. She said, "Oh yes," then opened a door to a room, gently pushed me in, and closed the door behind me. Inside the room was my dead mother, lying on a trolley by herself.

I was too late. I stood there, alone, looking at this body that was once my mother. But she wasn't there anymore. It became clear to me that I was looking at a shell, not a person. My mother had gone.

I waited there for a few minutes before walking out into the corridor to find the rest of my family in the day room.

At the funeral, my brother and I helped carry the coffin into the church.

My mother had a tough life. Six children, three strokes, divorced while she was ill and died at 67. I once asked if I could have her wedding ring as a keepsake when she died. She said no, and she never took it off. She was cremated with it on.

Janet helped me through it all, and within a few months, she had moved into my small cottage. Five years later, we were married. We still are.

Meditation

After 2–3 years in the school, you're gently pushed into taking up transcendental meditation.

> A BRAND NAME FOR A METHOD OF CALMING THE MIND AND BECOMING RELAXED BY SILENTLY REPEATING A SPECIAL WORD OR SERIES OF WORDS MANY TIMES
>
> CAMBRIDGE DICTIONARY

I was unsure about it. Was this going to mess with my head? Why were they pushing it? Maybe it was their way of taking over—you know, it was a cult, after all!

We had weeks of classes where the tutor kept telling us how wonderful it was, with ancient philosophers extolling its virtues.

> IT'S LIKE GOING HOME TO YOUR BEST FRIEND.
>
> SCHOOL TUTOR

Then came the ceremony! You had to bring flowers—five stems and a white handkerchief as an offering—and, of course, money!

I wasn't sure about this. I had already gained benefits from the school, like how I felt and thought—the "Exercise," the toolkit, "Not this, not this," "What would a wise person do. Why did I need more? So far, it was giving me what I was looking for, so maybe I should give them the benefit of the doubt."

The money "offering" was all the spare money you had in a month once all the bills were paid. You were essentially paying upfront for something you didn't know if you needed. It was also hinted that you couldn't continue at the school if you didn't go through with it. It all sounded a bit cultish.

We were told that in India, you'd have to serve your teacher for three years before being considered for meditation. So, we were lucky!

I travelled down to the school in Sheffield with the two Janets. The place was filled with silent, still members, showing you where to sit where to go, and offering cups of tea. The donation wasn't to the School of Philosophy but to the School of Meditation, an affiliate group.

You went into a room and presented the offerings—five stems, a white handkerchief, and an envelope with the money. The "Initiator" whispered the word that was to be repeated in your right ear. You repeated it out loud to ensure you had the pronunciation right, and then you meditated together for twenty minutes. After that, you went into a separate room to meditate for another thirty minutes.

It was a secret what you were supposed to pay, but I'll tell you—I paid £50.

I still feel like I cheated them.

I should have paid all the money I had in the bank. (it wasn't much)

Meditation is great. It's the best part of philosophy I've ever experienced.

PRINCIPLE THREE

"

THE SENSES ARE VERY FAST, AND THE MIND IS TURBULENT, RECEIVING IMPRESSIONS FROM DIFFERENT SOURCES. IT IS QUITE PROBABLE THAT SENSUAL HUNGER AND THIRST MAY BE INFLAMED BY THE BEAUTIFUL THINGS BEING SEEN IN THE WORLD, SO EVERY INDIVIDUAL NEEDS CONTROL OVER SENSORY APPETITE AND ITS EXPRESSION.

—SANATAN DHARMA
SHRI SANTANANDA SARASWATI, GOOD COMPANY (1987), THE STUDY SOCIETY

"

"

A MOST USEFUL APPROACH TO MEDITATION PRACTICE IS TO CONSIDER IT THE MOST IMPORTANT ACTIVITY OF EACH DAY. SCHEDULE IT AS YOU WOULD AN EXTREMELY IMPORTANT APPOINTMENT, AND UNFAILINGLY KEEP YOUR APPOINTMENT WITH THE INFINITE.

ROY EUGENE DAVIS

"

Here, I am extolling the virtues of meditation, and yet I don't practice what I preach. You're supposed to meditate for 30 minutes in the morning and evening, ideally at daybreak or sunset. I've never really done that. Even when I was attending classes at the school, I meditated only 2–3 times a week.

Still, there have been many times when I *needed* to meditate—when things got tough, or when I couldn't sleep. (Apparently, that's the wrong use of meditation. But it works)

Often, it's hard to meditate and hard to quiet the mind. But those are the times when you need it the most. Sometimes, it's just a relief.

I know wives who've never been part of the school, but they send their husbands off to meditate when things get difficult.

It's the best tool I have.

Once, after a 30-minute meditation session, I described my internal organs as having dropped three inches in my body from relaxing.

I truly believe stress is a huge killer. Meditation helps more than any drug. It allows you to *really* think—not just repeat the same circling thoughts.

“

QUIET THE MIND, AND THE SOUL WILL SPEAK.

MA JAYA SATI BHAGAVATI

”

“

MEDITATION IS NOT ABOUT STOPPING THOUGHTS BUT RECOGNISING THAT WE ARE MORE THAN OUR THOUGHTS AND OUR FEELINGS.

ARIANNA HUFFINGTON

”

Great quote. We attach ourselves to our thoughts and feelings so much that we think we’ll always be in the mood we’re currently in. But moods and feelings change. The reality is that peace of mind is always there—it never goes away. *We* go away.

“

REMEMBER THE BLUE SKY. IT MAY AT TIMES BE OBSCURED BY CLOUDS, BUT IT IS ALWAYS THERE.

ANDY PUDDICOMBE

”

“

WHEN MEDITATION IS MASTERED, THE MIND IS UNWAVERING LIKE THE FLAME OF A CANDLE IN A WINDLESS PLACE.

BHAGAVAD GITA

”

Mastering the mind—that's something I haven't achieved yet, but it's the road I want to be on. I want to be the master of my mind, not the other way around. I am responsible, not some automatic reaction based on flawed visions of past experiences.

But I digress. Back to Holdsworth's.

I was still at Holdsworth's. The factory was now running as it should—productivity and quality were good. There were no more dismissals or court cases. The mill's management team of planners and supervisors was one of the best I'd ever worked with. I'd done all I could there. I couldn't get promoted because the brother was in the way.

Then, I got a call from a head-hunter looking for a mill manager in Littleborough. I listened. I had a meeting with the owner, and within an hour, the deal was done. I left Holdsworth's—to the dismay of Michael and the team, but I think to the relief of the Operations Director, who got his job back.

Looking back, I see my time at Holdsworth's as a turning point. I'd managed a company turnaround, started studying philosophy, met and started living with Janet (my future wife), began my MBA, and found my confidence by getting through tough times.

So, what did I do with my newfound freedom? I left the School of Philosophy, of course.

What's the point of finding myself if I can't do good for society? Was it just for me? I needed to be good and do good things. Where is the hardest place to do good? The Samaritans.

The Samaritans are a charity that focuses on listening to people who are at the end of the road—those who are suicidal, those who can't cope any longer, or people who just need someone to listen. The key is they don't tell people *not* to commit suicide. They give people the opportunity to discuss it without judgment.

With my MBA, work, my daughter, and the School of Philosophy, something had to give for me to do good and help others. So, I gave up the School of Philosophy. I thought I'd learned enough, but I was wrong.

It was tough—three-hour sessions, overnight shifts, waiting for the phone to ring. You never knew who was on the line or what was going to happen. Some calls lasted seconds, some hours. Some were frivolous, others harrowing.

After a year away from the school, I asked to go back. Why? Because my spiritual well was dry. I needed to be reminded of the truth and freedom in life. I'd gotten too caught up in the world.

I ended up doing three years with the Samaritans—the average is two. I did my best, but in some cases, that probably wasn't good enough.

CHAPTER TEN

FOTHERGILL ENGINEERED FABRICS (FEF)

FEF was part of a group with its main site in Littleborough and satellite locations in Rochdale and Ealees. There was another large building in Oldham, which housed three additional companies: one making fire blankets, another producing raincoat material, and the third manufacturing rubber parts for the car industry. The jewel of the group was Fothergill Coated Fabrics (FCF), the smallest site located in Rochdale, where Teflon-coated fabrics were produced. Despite the scale of these operations, the total turnover for all these companies was no more than £20 million.

I was the Manufacturing Manager at FEF. We specialised in technical woven mineral fabric and the weaving of Kevlar, used for bulletproof vests. Remarkably, the company had one of the few bulletproof testing departments in the country—an entirely new experience for me. The people at the site spoke a strange dialect, and although it was only eleven miles away, it felt like I had stepped into a different world. It was like going back in time to the old industrial mills of yesteryear. Overall, the people on the shop floor were generally nice, some of the management were a bit dubious.

I should have realised what I was getting into when, before my first day, the owner invited me to dinner in Hebden Bridge to share his thoughts on the management. He was an Irishman who flew from Cork every Monday to work and returned on Friday. During the week, he stayed at a local pub. Not a great idea.

Back to basics: I set production targets, began replacing outdated weaving machines, reorganised the shop floor, and worked on boosting morale. Six months later, I was promoted to Corporate Manufacturing Manager, overseeing five sites and three companies, essentially serving as the group's Operations Director.

On my first day at the Oldham site, I was greeted with a letter from the Health and Safety Executive (HSE), warning that unless immediate action was taken over the number of serious incidents, the site would be closed. Here we go. I had no prior knowledge of these issues, but I had to act quickly.

We called in the HSE and developed a plan. The General Manager of the Oldham site looked the part, talked the part but could not do the part. He was also a friend of the owner, which complicated things. Despite being nice enough, I think he sensed that my presence meant his demise. I was put in charge over him. So, it was me who had to sack him.

I went to the site on a Friday at 4 p.m., and I called him into the office. I told him that unless he could provide a good reason not to make him redundant by 8 a.m. Monday morning, I would make him redundant. I offered him a year's salary and an extra £500 to consult with a solicitor, provided he signed a compromise agreement stating he wouldn't take the company to court. By Monday at 8 a.m., he could not think of a reason. I actually think he had had enough, so he accepted the offer and he was gone.

I was soon invited to join the group's governing board, which included two directors from Sales, the Finance Director, the owner, and myself as Operations Director. I signed cheques that appeared on insurance documents, and company letterheads. Maybe I had made it!

Money was always tight in the company. We were factoring sales and constantly trying to refinance the company, holding meetings with all the major banks and even some smaller ones. Any excess funds went into FCF, they coated glass fabric with PTFE, expensive but highly profitable, which was a new venture. It was the owner's pride and joy, but making it all work was challenging.

Getting across all five sites and attending local and group meetings was exhausting. The most difficult site to get the required improvements in place was in Oldham, where the mindset seemed trapped in the 18th century, particularly concerning health and safety, working conditions, and employee treatment. The Oldham site was a large Victorian mill, just off the M60. The owner had bought it a year earlier from its previous owners, who still held the property and leased it out, but sold the businesses. They had never spent any money on the buildings in the past—even now they didn't. The businesses, though made money. The previous owner used to just to come in his flash car and expensive suit every now and then to tell me I was doing everything wrong. Thanks for that.

The rubber compounding company made sure the entire building was covered in a layer of carbon black dust. It looked awful. The people who worked in the compounding plant looked like they had just emerged from a mine. Health and safety standards were either non-existent or ignored entirely. Both management and employees seemed not to care.

Another company at the site produced rubber-coated fabric for the production of raincoats, with high-profile clients like Burberry, Chanel, and other top fashion houses. The machines and workers were old and grimy. The employees worked on a low basic wage, topped up with a good piece rate system. They used a solvent called toluene as part of the vulcanisation process. The Toluene cost £0.50/ kg to the company, but was sold at £5/bag in Oldham, illegally in empty crisp packets to sniff.

One night, two young men climbed onto the roof to try and break in to steal some toluene. One of them fell through the roof and broke his back, while the other managed to siphon a bucket of toluene from the tank, and hide it outside the factory wall next to the canal, to be picked up later, before calling an ambulance. The police and ambulance arrived, taking the man with the broken back to hospital and the other man to the police station. The next day, the HSE arrived, not to address the theft, but to try and prosecute the company for having an unsafe roof!

The rubber coating department had a cat that, to my eyes, was permanently high from the solvent fumes. It slept on his own chair in the filthy office with punk hair. If you tried to stroke the cat, as if you would, you would receive a nasty scratch for your efforts. The two managers in charge of the department were paid well but looked like they had been begging on the streets. They tolerated me, but knowing full well, like I did, that they made good profits and would likely be left alone. They also made fabric for the fetish industry. Every now and then, I would see shiny black, fluorescent green or orange fabric being produced. For these customers, the trick was not to cure the rubber properly as the smell of uncured rubber that the fetish customers wanted.

Toward the end of my time with the company, I received a visit from the local council. They wanted to close the factory, claiming it was an eyesore and did not reflect the area that they were trying to make into a high-tech industrial estate. They were right. When I informed, the owner swore me to secrecy. A few years later, I noticed the mill was gone.

One of the offshoots of FEF was in a building in Rochdale that housed a sewing unit and air jet looms. The air jets required a clean environment, which they couldn't get in the main mill. The sewing section sewed the mineral loose woven fabric into bags for the aluminium industry to be used as filters. This was challenging because the open mesh fabric was difficult to sew, and we began to struggle to keep up with demand and start losing sewers due to the difficulty of the work.

We had a customer in Thailand who was purchasing the PTFE coated fabric produced by the FCF company. The owner and sales director decided we could set up a factory in Thailand to produce the bags, so I was sent to Bangkok with a week's notice.

I was told to look for a Swiss guy who resembled an Arab at the airport—our customer, who was supposed to help me. I was worried that I wouldn't recognise him but the moment I got through customs, there he was—he looked exactly like a Swiss Arab!

I had arranged to go to the British embassy to discuss how they could help us in finding a business partner or getting support for starting a company in Thailand. Unfortunately, they weren't much help. Their primary message was to avoid corruption at all costs: "If you get involved in any type of corruption you will, you'll go to prison in Thailand or the UK." A few weeks later, some of our material got held up at Bangkok airport, and our agent quietly paid an extra fee to get it released.

When I met with the Thai authorities, the atmosphere was stern and serious—until a film crew appeared. Suddenly, there were tea and biscuits, and the officials had smiling faces as I agreed to be part of a government advert to attract more foreign business. Apparently, I was on local TV that night.

I travelled around Bangkok but quickly realised our operation was too small to justify setting up our own production unit. It was better to buy some capacity. Travelling around with some of the managers of the industrial estates, you could feel the corruption, never asked for but certainly inferred.

In the evenings, Martin, the Swiss guy, would take me out for food and drinks. Everywhere we went, there were girls waiting to serve us. Sex again was not overt but inferred. Girls wore denim shorts and tight tops, and we would sit in bars, watching the world go by, trying to guess which women were real and which were "ladyboys." The giveaway was that the lady boys had big tits and an Adam's apple.

I enjoy a good massage, and in Bangkok, a two-hour session cost around £5. However, you were always offered a "happy ending" for extra. I was too embarrassed. I was a lad from a council estate in Bradford.

One night, Martin introduced me to another Swiss guy who worked for a shipment company that I would need to send the material back to the UK. He assured me we were going to a smart restaurant with no funny business. We arrived, and standing outside were two beautiful Thai girls in traditional dress, welcoming us. "This looks good," I thought. I sat on a stool at the bar for drinks, but within five minutes, there were two of us on the seat—a beautiful Thai girl and me. Martin and his friend also had girls, and they seemed very happy.

She told me about her life in good English, explaining how she sent money back to her family. After an hour, I gave her the equivalent of £10 to leave, much to the disgust of my two colleagues, who felt obliged to let their hostesses go as well.

We went on to play snooker at a new hospitality club. The place was well-equipped with pool and snooker tables, large TV screens, and a bar. Behind the bar, there were a group of ladies in a line for you to choose which one you wanted. Not for me. I think I'm shy.

The locals tried to explain that my unease about the sex on offer was misplaced. Most of the time, it was just hospitality. Taking a woman to bed was certainly on offer, but it would have been expensive. There's no divorce in Thailand; a husband can just walk away, often leaving the wife destitute. This leads to women turning to "hospitality."

As it was explained to me, these women go to the hairdresser, put on makeup, wear nice clothes, and work to earn some money for their families. To deny them this would be worse than accepting their hospitality. There are always two sides to every story. Unfortunately, my working-class morality and belief that women are at least equal to men was never overcome.

PRINCIPLE SEVEN

> "ONE IS EXPECTED TO USE ONE'S INTELLECT OR REASON AND FIND OUT THE CAUSES OF THINGS AND USE THEM AS NECESSITY MAY RISE.
>
> SANATAN DHARMA, SHRI SHANTANANDA SARASWATI, "

Eventually, I visited a sewing company in Bangkok owned by a Chinese family. (Many of the businesses are owned by Chinese families, and around 30% of the population are Chinese). They were interested in producing the bags.

The next time I visited Thailand, the company allowed me to take my new partner, Janet. She loved it. As I worked at looking at other sites and getting closer to the Chinese sewing company, she went sightseeing. As it was off-season, she often had a limousine and a guide all to herself.

We always stayed in a four-star hotel in the business district, away from the seedier areas—or so I thought. One day, Janet went to the basement for a facial, and while waiting, I decided to get a massage. There was only a thin wall between us. My massage was going well until the masseuse started paying more attention to one particular area. She asked if she could make me happy. I said, "My girlfriend is next door." She replied, "She will never know." I said, "No, but I WILL."

She then said, "My name is Oi. If you want me, just call Oi." I thought you couldn't make this up! I quickly dressed, went next door, gave Janet some money for her treatment, and told her I'd meet her upstairs.

At the weekend, Janet and I hired the hotel concierge's brother to drive us to Pattaya for the day. We were there during the day, walking about.

As we walked the streets, we sensed what the atmosphere would be like at night. There were large bars without walls, with girls waiting for the punters to arrive. We received some funny looks from older Scandinavian or German men in their 60s or 70s, walking along the seafront hand in hand with teenage Thai girls. I am not sure they would know what "Coals to Newcastle" meant, but they certainly looked like they were thinking something similar.

Martin's business partner in Thailand was also the leader of the Harley Davidson motorcycle club. He arranged some tickets for us to see the Rolling Stones in Bangkok, but the band pulled out the day before the concert due to SARS. Pity.

Eventually, I set up a contract with the Chinese company to produce the bags. I sent two of our best sewing operatives to Bangkok to teach their workers how to make the bags. The women from Rochdale were much less squeamish than me. They asked to be taken to a show where women performed tricks, shooting ping pong balls out of a certain orifice, which I think I should leave to your imagination.

Even with transporting the raw material to Thailand, having the bags produced there, and shipping them back, we reduced the cost of manufacturing by half.

Meanwhile, things weren't going so well with FCF. The cost of the building, repayments on new machinery, and quality issues led to it becoming unfeasible.

The owner called me in and told me the factory had to shut down. I contacted a local security company. That night, at around seven o'clock, I went to the factory with the security guards and told the night shift to pack up and go home; the factory was closing. There were around five or six people on-site, and they acted with the utmost dignity. They asked if they could clean the machines down before stopping, as PTFE liquid, once set, becomes like concrete. I agreed. They cleaned and left. We changed all the locks and put a security man in the building, who came with his girlfriend, and that was it. It was in receivership.

The owner took it hard. He retreated to his office and, I genuinely think, into a bottle, and we hardly got anything out of him for 3-4 months. The other parts of the business still needed to run, so I stepped in and made the necessary decisions, which caused me a lot of stress. Everyone wanted to know what was going on.

I had negotiated a pay raise with the employees at FEF over the last few months, but I called in all the union leaders and not only reneged on the agreed pay deal but also closed the final salary pension scheme and announced a 10% redundancy. Their choice was to accept the terms or see the company close, with everyone out of a job.

I noticed the board was changing as well. First, the financial director was dismissed, and then the two sales directors. Before long, I wasn't the newest member of the board but the oldest.

Eventually, the owner bought FCF back from the receivers and started again. He came out of his office and looked at what was happening. He was not happy. He said I was trying to take over his company; I said he was a lot better owner when he was sober.

I was exhausted. I went on holiday, and while I was away, he sent me a letter telling me not to come back. Two months later, we met on neutral ground at a restaurant in Shaw. He told me there had been many allegations against me from some employees. I responded by saying, "Okay, let's go to court for unfair dismissal and sort it out. I'm happy to defend myself."

Before I went on holiday, I had appeared, I think, tired and uncommunicative, but now I was ready and happy to fight anyone and anything. He told me he would throw so much mud that some of it would stick. I said, "Bring it on."

We looked at each other for a moment before he said, “You’ve been away too long; you can’t go back.” I agreed. It was too late. At this point, it was all about the compensation.

He offered me six months’ wages and a great reference, which I could ask for anytime. I accepted, and we parted on good terms. If I had not been so bullish, I would not have gotten what I thought was a good deal. From what I gathered later, all those who had spoken against me were dismissed within six months.

This was the first time I had been sacked, although all the paperwork said “redundant.” I felt like a failure. I learned a lot, but in the end, I think the only thing I achieved was keeping a struggling business afloat.

It had been tough. I’d completed my MBA, but I never managed to get to grips with the production issues because I was spread too thin and had no money to spend. I had reneged on deals with the workforce, sacked people, and shut down factories.

Maybe I lived by the sword and died by it.

I had begun teaching philosophy at Huddersfield while still attending my own classes in Leeds. We discussed some of the situations I was experiencing at work. Some students disagreed with how I’d behaved. They thought I was using philosophy as an excuse or as a support for the bad decisions I was making.

That made me think.

Philosophy and Career

Definition:

> THE JOB OR SERIES OF JOBS THAT YOU DO DURING YOUR WORKING LIFE, ESPECIALLY IF YOU CONTINUE TO GET BETTER JOBS AND EARN MORE MONEY.
>
> CAMBRIDGE DICTIONARY

My career has had its ups and downs, from being an apprentice to a Group Manufacturing Manager, General Manager, and Group Business Excellence Manager. I never reached the Director or Vice President level. Maybe that was a good thing? Maybe I just did not have the patience to wait for things to change.

When I became bored or felt I'd hit a ceiling, I acted. I always have. I gather as much data as I can, make an informed decision, and then act. But did I act for myself, for other people, or for the company I was working for?

"

HE IS A CHARISMATIC LEADER WHO INSPIRES PEOPLE TO FOLLOW HIM. A STRATEGIC THINKER WHO CAN MASTER THE DETAILS. A TIRELESS WORKER WITH INCREDIBLE FOCUS AND PROBLEM-SOLVING SKILLS. HE IS WELL-LIKED BY HIS EMPLOYEES BUT IS ALSO ABLE TO MAKE AND EXECUTE UNPOPULAR DECISIONS. ABOVE ALL, HE IS AN EXCEPTIONAL COMMUNICATOR WHO CAN CONVEY A VISION TO ANY AUDIENCE, FROM WALL STREET TO THE MOST JUNIOR EMPLOYEE."

JACK MCCULLOUGH
DECEMBER EDITION OF *FORBES* MAGAZINE

"

In December's edition of Forbes magazine, Jack McCullough uses this as a description of a corporate psychopath.

I would have been proud if someone had described me this way, but this is a description of a corporate psychopath. Maybe I am a psychopath?

Experts say people with psychopathy crave power and dominant positions. They are also chameleons, able to disguise their ruthlessness and antisocial behaviour under the veneer of charm and eloquence. In extreme clinical cases, these traits have allowed serial killers to elude capture.

Is this me? Am I a psychopath? Cool.

I never enjoyed making those difficult decisions—I can lead a team, I can inspire, I can be tireless, and I always have a vision. But does that mean I am a psychopath?

I generally support the left of politics but seem to have spent many years fighting the unions. This will continue in future roles. Do I use philosophy as a mask, an excuse to hide my desire for power?

I have worked with many great teams over the years, and some were quite upset when I decided to leave. A few team members didn't speak to me again until after I had left. Was it all just a hunger for power?

Tomas Chamorro-Premuzic, a professor of business psychology at University College London and Columbia University and an associate at Harvard's Entrepreneurial Finance Lab, suggests that 20% of business leaders are psychopaths. Am I one of them? He provides three ways of spotting a psychopath or narcissist:

1. ***They* often *crave validation and recognition from others. This* is primarily because *their* self-esteem is *high but fragile. Bosses who constantly show off are* probably *desperate for* others' *admiration.***

   No, I don't do that. In fact, I take praise badly. It's hard to show off if you look like me.

2. ***They tend to be self-centred.*** **This means they're generally less interested** ***in others and*** **have deficits in** ***empathy. For this reason, they*** **are** ***rarely*** **found displaying any** ***genuine*** **consideration** ***for people*** **other than** ***themselves.***

   Nope, I spent four years as a Samaritan, and I cry at every sad film. Then again, I am writing this book...

3. ***They have high levels of entitlement. Narcissists*** **commonly** ***behave as if they deserve certain privileges or enjoy higher status than their peers*** **enjoy.**

   No, I don't think so... Well, no, I'm pretty sure.

So, no. I don't think I'm a psychopath. No, I'm sure, really.

But how do I justify the redundancies, dismissals, and strife that I've inflicted on so many people?

> “
>
> YOUR CAREER IS YOUR OWN RESPONSIBILITY. YOUR EMPLOYER IS NOT YOUR MOTHER.
>
> JURGEN APPELO
>
> ”

This is a start. I have never thought that my future was in the hands of my employers. Oh sure, I worry and have sleepless nights about things I've said, done, or failed to do and about what other people think. I have never been rich enough not to care about the future. But my career, my future, is up to me.

> "I AM NOT THE PRODUCT OF MY CIRCUMSTANCES. I AM A PRODUCT OF MY DECISIONS.
>
> STEPHEN COVEY"

It's my fault—no one else's. I had a tough childhood, but it doesn't define me. My mistakes, and there have been many, are mine. I'm not a victim of fate or a madman running the company. When I'd had enough, I left. Usually of my own accord, though not always. Sometimes, I jumped from the frying pan into the fire—that was my mistake.

By the way, I've also had successes.

“

WRITE YOUR OWN BOOK INSTEAD OF READING SOMEONE ELSE'S BOOK ABOUT SUCCESS

HERB BROOKS

”

If you remember, philosophy is about making wise decisions. So, make your own decisions.

People come into your life; some stay for a long time, some for only a short while, but they all help make up your story. Still, it's your story. The people I dismissed, made redundant, hired, promoted, or trained—I was part of their story for a time, but it remains their story, not mine.

“

EVERY ACTION HAS A CONSEQUENCE, SO ALWAYS TRY TO BE GOOD.

RICHARD EYRE

”

Absolutely. Try to be good. I have always tried to do the right thing. Even when I ended up being wrong, my intention was to do what I thought was right.

I believe in karma—in this life, never mind the next.

Karma:

> THE PRINCIPLE OF RETRIBUTIVE JUSTICE DETERMINING A PERSON'S STATE OF LIFE AND THEIR REINCARNATIONS AS THE EFFECT OF PAST DEEDS.
>
> COLLINS DICTIONARY

So, long story short, I made those decisions because I believed it was right to do so at the time. Whether it turned out to be right or wrong doesn't matter. I did what I thought was right at the time.

I support British manufacturing. I believe in making it more efficient, generating more profit, and creating jobs for people. I believe in employment and in people having the freedom to spend their hard-earned money as they choose. If I had to make a few people redundant to keep many more employed, I would do it. If a manager was putting people's livelihoods at risk, *I would take action.*

Naïve? Idealistic, perhaps. I had a job to do, and I did it to the best of my ability. Maybe I was trying to be the

Philosopher King? Or maybe I'm just kidding myself, but thoughts like these can lead you to disappear up your own arsehole.

"

BE YOURSELF, EVERYONE ELSE IS ALREADY TAKEN.

OSCAR WILDE

"

CHAPTER ELEVEN

BACK TO INTERFACE

I was a bit battered and bruised after being sacked at FEF. I began the usual process of sending out CVs and applications. After a few weeks, one of the agencies I'd contacted about a particular job phoned to ask if I'd be interested in returning to Interface. This was a company, technology, and industry I knew well, so I said yes. Steve Martin, who had once been my rival, was now, ten years later, the Site Director. He asked me to come in for an interview with him and the European Vice President, Ton Van Keken, for the role of Operations Manager.

When I arrived for the interview, I noticed it had changed over the last ten years. The two-needle punch departments were gone, the office block looked quite plush, and they had a nice new canteen. Before the interview, they asked if I wanted to join them for lunch in the canteen. I declined—having lunch with the interviewers before the interview seemed odd to me.

The interview itself wasn't great because *I* was not great. I was lacking confidence or whatever, and to top it all off, I even forgot what 5S stood for! I explained what I'd been doing over the past decade, and they filled me in on what had been happening at the company. Peter Edwards, the previous manager, was still there, but he wanted a break from the day-to-day firing line. They were looking for someone with a more modern approach.

I got the job, mostly because Steve wanted me back. I am not sure Ton was thrilled about it, but I was glad to return to work in something that technologically I knew well.

On my first day, I was greeted in the car park by the Personnel Manager, who welcomed me back. Then he said that not everyone was happy about it. Good. Great start!

One major issue at the time was an ongoing industrial dispute. For once, this was one I had not started. The company was American-owned, and they had a tough year financially, so they imposed a global pay freeze. Although the UK operation performed reasonably well, the freeze was still applied. Naturally, the union objected, leading to a one-day strike. The head of the union had stood outside the factory gates on the picket line. Steve went outside and served an injunction on the union and, so the strike was called off, but an overtime ban and work-to-rule were enforced. Although the company was not a closed shop, everyone on the shop floor, about 100 people, were members. This had all happened six months before I arrived.

The factory's morale was at rock bottom, and nothing was being done to resolve the dispute. UK management's hands were tied by the US owners.

There were clear signs of the union's strength within the factory. The main machine was a bitumen backing carpet line. Rolls of tufted carpet were produced in Northern Ireland, and these were then transported to the factory at Shelf, where bitumen backing was applied and then cut into tiles. This machine ran on three shifts, needed thirteen people to operate, and ran at 7m/hr. This speed had been agreed with the union, as they said you could not inspect the tiles quicker than that. Besides the bitumen backing line, there was a latex line, a fusion bonded department with pleaters and slitters, a PVC compounding plant, a PVC backing line, and a jet printer. However, the jet print business and fusion bonded products were in decline. By far, the most important machine was the bitumen backing line.

The smoking area was situated in the main corridor between the offices and the factory—apparently because they did not want it to be outside because it was cold. The factory itself was dirty, dusty, and untidy, processing fifty tonnes of limestone a day to add weight to the bitumen backing.

I tried to stay clear of the dispute, but little by little, I was dragged in. I wanted to apply lean manufacturing to the site, but with the work-to-rule there was no appetite for it. The company did not want to start training or anything else until the dispute was resolved.

Eventually, after discussions with the MD, Steve, and HR, I opened a dialogue with the union. I invited the Branch Chairman, Secretary, and the four shop stewards for a meeting. I offered to give more in sick pay and a review of the bonus scheme. I pointed out that there were only four months left until the next round of pay negotiations, which the company would look favourably at the pay rise.

They were very polite and thanked me for the offer. But it wasn't me, they said. They had had enough of the dispute too, but they could not go back to the members without securing a pay rise after all the turmoil.

The die was cast.

The overall orders were down, and the sister plant in Holland had more capacity than they were currently using. We announced that we were reducing operations to two shifts, which meant a redundancy programme, with at least twenty jobs to be cut.

It was just before Christmas. We developed redundancy criteria based on length of service, skills, absenteeism, and warnings. If morale could get any lower, it did.

Both Steve and I received anonymous Christmas cards, wishing that they hoped we would be visited by three ghosts to help us mend our evil ways. I stuck mine up on the noticeboard with a thank-you note.

When meeting with the local full-time union official, he said the HR was listening to their arguments against the redundancy programme, but Steve and I were not. They were right. I felt sorry for the union representatives. They could not go back to the union members when there had been such efforts with little or nothing. But this dispute was threatening the future of the entire site.

Eventually, the redundancy programme was rolled out. I carried out the dismissals with Steve to hear the appeals. No one appealed.

Those people caught up in the redundancies were the Union Branch Secretary, Chairman and two of the four shop stewards. Another shop steward resigned due to stress.

The remaining shop steward called for a vote, and it was passed by the members to end the overtime ban and the work-to-rule.

I walked to the bitumen backing line after the vote and turned the speed dial to as high as I could on the bitumen backing line. I then spent 2-3 hours inspecting the carpet tiles myself to ensure that it could be done, and that was it. Productivity increased by 15%.

Being an American company based in Georgia, a real republican area, the industrial dispute had caused untold damage to the reputation. In their eyes it was a problem site now.

There was going to be little to no investment for us. Instead, the money went to the sister site in Holland, where it was more expensive to dismiss workers, there was no history of industrial strife, and it was easier to supply products to the European market.

From this point on, whatever we achieved would be down to us.

Where to begin? First, show your face. Get out on the factory floor. The workers thought that the company had beaten them. They had lost. Smile, encourage, say well done to the smallest thing.

The old bonus system had paid nothing or little for the past couple of years. Together with Steve, I worked on developing a new bonus scheme. The old one had paid out little to nothing for the past few years. The new scheme was based on reducing costs and saving material, and Interface had always been at the forefront of sustainability. Sustainability is easy to sell if you can emphasise the benefits to the community and financial rewards. The new bonus could pay out up to £800 per quarter if we saved on labour and materials against the budget. We made the targets clear, and I put up a big board in the factory, showing our progress with smiley or frowning faces depending on whether we hit our goals. We set up meetings with the workforce so they could run projects on how to achieve their bonuses.

We also began cleaning up the factory. In lean methodology, you are supposed to create a 5S committee to run the programme. I gathered the shift managers, Quality Director, Planning Managers, Engineering Director, HR and some others who had shown interest. At the meeting, I outlined the commitment and determination required, emphasising the benefits we could expect. I was passionate—I believed in this. I walked around the room, encouraging everyone to share my vision.

Two days later, I got a call from HR. Some of the attendees were uneasy with the passion and determination; could I tone it down?

No.

That was the end of the committee. However, two or three people at the meeting got it. One was a female planner named Emma. I asked Steve for a Continuous Improvement Coordinator to help with the changes I wanted to implement. He agreed, and after interviews,

Emma got the job—much to the Planning Director's disgust.

Women often make the best CI people. They want things clean and in order, and they're unthreatening. Emma was also intelligent and good-looking, which helps when dealing with a predominantly male workforce. It might sound misogynistic, but it's true.

Emma was great. She became like my work wife—with all the good bits of trust and support but none of the messy bits. Oh, we sometimes argued, but not often, and we did good things.

Next up: start the training.

I brought in a training company from Yorkshire led by Paul, the MD. He was great at organising government funding support, and we trained the team in NVQ Level 2 and 3 Manufacturing Techniques. Paul was great, a very good communicator. He once brought in a Formula Ford racing car into the factory to demonstrate quick changeover times with the wheels, like in Formula 1. The whole thing was filmed so we could play it back to make improvements.

The union rep did not want to be filmed doing anything with the company. Understandably, feelings were still raw after the dispute.

After about 20 minutes of the guys trying to work out how to undo the wheel nuts, the shop steward shouted, "You're doing it all wrong!" He jumped in front of the camera and began using the pneumatic drill to remove the wheel.

Stopping the production lines to carry out the training has an amazing effect. The shop floor workers usually think management only cares about the production (which we do, but no need to let them know that). Taking time to stop the machines for training, have a bit of fun, and work towards certificates they could add to their CVs, while working on projects that led to improved bonuses, helped lift morale.

For the next two years, productivity increased every month.

Part of the training involved 5S, which stands for Sort, set in Order, Shine, Standardise, and Sustain—a Toyota Production System method for improving housekeeping. Many people assume 5S is just about keeping things tidy, but it is so much more: it fosters pride, responsibility, and ownership of where you work. Making it a clean and safe place to work. 5S is a fundamental culture change.

I was on a trip to our tufting factory, which was on a shared industrial estate in Craigavon, Northern Ireland, where there was a nice-looking glass bus shelter in the shared car park of the industrial estate. I mentioned it to Tony, the manager of the site, and he sent a forklift to pick it up. We loaded it onto one of the many lorries heading back to Shelf. Three days later, we had installed a new smoking shelter outside the building, demolished the interior structure and painted all around it. I still wonder who owned that shelter in Craigavon... but not often.

The new bonus scheme paid out well, and the site was making good money. Customer orders increased to the point where we had to create a night shift. Gradually, I built it out of temporary labour because the existing workforce still did not fully trust us and thought we might replace them with temps. But soon, the night shift was outperforming the double day shift, and we gradually put all the temps on permanent contracts based on their performance.

It was time to make the night shift permanent, so I brought in one of my shift managers from Holdsworth's, Anton. We began the 12-week notice period to change the contracts to rotating shifts. It was not easy, but everyone stayed.

At this point, we were either running the bitumen line or the PVC line. If I could figure out how to run both at the same time without increasing labour costs, I knew I could make the site more profitable.

Hmmm.

I looked at the Print and Fusion Bonded departments, which were not fully loaded. I decided to train them to run the PVC line. Some of them weren't happy, as they saw themselves as a step above operatives—which, in many cases, was probably true, but they could see their orders were declining.

After a few weeks of training in the main area, I had the latex line, bitumen backing line, and PVC backing line all working at the same time for one day a week.

It felt good. The factory was clean, direct labour costs were down, quality was good, and Overall Equipment Efficiency (OEE) was strong.

This caused problems with our Dutch colleagues. The carpet itself was tufted in Craigavon, Northern Ireland, and then sent to Shelf for backing. Any excess material we could not process went to Holland to be backed on their bitumen line. As the Shelf became more efficient, less material was sent to Scherpenzeel, where their factory was situated. By manipulating the workforce to run both lines at once, even less material was going to Holland. Good for us, bad for them. I didn't tell them the plan... oops!

We had quarterly meetings as a European Operations group led by Ton. I enjoyed them. Our numbers were good, so I was happy to share. Most of the meetings were in Shelf or Scherpenzeel, but we would also go to some of the sales centres and have some meetings there. Barcelona was good, as were Utrecht, Copenhagen, and Amsterdam. There were always activities—cycling around the canals in Amsterdam, which was fun (I even broke one of the pedals). Wine tasting in Utrecht, where I was standing with Tony from Craigavon, who only drank Guinness and kept passing the wine samples to me. Cheers, Tony.

Munich was good. Tony and I ended up in an Irish bar (naturally) where they were showing the Rugby Union match between England and South Africa on the big screen. The place was packed with supporters, all decked out in their team's gold shirts. Before the game, they played the national anthems. The South Africans sang theirs with full force, and when England's turn came, there was silence. I wasn't having that, so I stood on a chair and belted out "God Save the Queen" as loud as I could. Tony, being a Catholic from Northern Ireland, declined to sing and looked away. I got one or two comments, but I was well on the way by then.

England were crushed. It was embarrassing, much to the amusement of the South African supporters. To be fair, I did not buy another drink that night—the South African fans kept buying them for me, with a chuckle and a slap on the back.

The Dutch were generally a little more stand-offish. The guys from Shelf and Northern Ireland saw these trips as a chance to share best practice, find out what's going on and have a bit of fun, while the Dutch took a more reserved, Lutheran approach—except for Ton, who to be fair, saw it as a way to let off some steam.

One of the Dutch Operations Managers, Bert Bleaker, was someone I got along with well. He was younger than me, a typical Dutchman—tall and well-built. He had a wife and two young kids. I went over once with Emma to look at some of the things he was doing in his factory and shamed him out that night instead of going home. Something I regret because six months later, he was diagnosed with terminal cancer.

There was nothing they could do. We talked on the phone a few times, and he was shocked and did not know what to do. I did not even know what to say except to fight with everything he had. He died. I went to his funeral in Holland. It was an open casket. The steroids had bloated him, and he didn't look like the Bert I knew. His wife and two children sat next to the coffin. It was terrible. That was 15-16 years ago.

Recently, I buried my eldest sister. It snowed, and it was freezing as they lowered her coffin into the ground. I'm not good with funerals.

Adventures with Death

"

I AM NOT FRIGHTENED OF DYING. ANY TIME WILL DO. I DON'T MIND. WHY SHOULD I MIND? THERE'S NO REASON FOR IT. YOU'VE GOT TO GO SOMETIME.

PINK FLOYD
THE GREAT GIG IN THE SKY

"

I wish I could be as cavalier about death as Pink Floyd describes. They're absolutely right, of course. The one thing that's certain when you are born is that you will die. With that in mind, I do not want to be afraid of it.

"

I CANNOT ESCAPE DEATH, BUT AT LEAST I CAN ESCAPE THE FEAR OF IT.

EPICTETUS

"

But how do you escape that fear? Reason helps, but it's not always enough. I once had kidney stones, and people told me you could meditate the pain away. I tried and failed. It hurt. Also, like the fear of death, you can try and reason it away, but it still lingers. I do not want a fear.

“

WHAT UPSETS PEOPLE IS NOT THINGS THEMSELVES BUT THEIR JUDGMENTS ABOUT THE THINGS. FOR EXAMPLE, DEATH IS NOTHING DREADFUL (OR ELSE IT WOULD HAVE APPEARED DREADFUL TO SOCRATES), BUT INSTEAD THE JUDGMENT ABOUT DEATH THAT IT IS DREADFUL—THAT IS WHAT IS DREADFUL. SO, WHEN WE ARE THWARTED OR UPSET OR DISTRESSED, LET US NEVER BLAME SOMEONE ELSE BUT RATHER OURSELVES, THAT IS, OUR OWN JUDGMENTS.

AN UNEDUCATED PERSON ACCUSES OTHERS WHEN HE IS DOING BADLY; A PARTLY EDUCATED PERSON ACCUSES HIMSELF, AN EDUCATED PERSON ACCUSES NEITHER SOMEONE ELSE NOR HIMSELF.

EPICTETUS

”

From this quote, I can see that I am only partly educated—I blame myself rather than others. Still more work to do. Again, this quote strikes true. Death is neither good nor bad; it just *is*. We should not fear it because fear of the inevitable is pointless.

I recently watched the film, "A *Bridge of Spies*" with Tom Hanks and the British actor Sir Mark Rylance, who played the Russian spy Rudolf Abel. In the film, Tom Hanks keeps asking Sir Mark if he is worried about maybe being executed in the US or shot on his return to the USSR; he replies, **"Will it help?"** Wonderful. Does worrying about death help? What benefit is there in it? Does worrying about anything help? In fact, ask yourself the question, "When has worrying ever helped"? You suffer twice, once worrying and then if the event actually happens. Dealing with the present moment does not include fear. The worst that can happen is that you can die. Once you accept that, fear has nothing to cling to.

"

DO NOT ACT AS IF YOU HAD TEN THOUSAND YEARS TO THROW AWAY. DEATH STANDS AT YOUR ELBOW. BE GOOD FOR SOMETHING WHILE YOU LIVE AND IT IS IN YOUR POWER.

MARCUS AURELIUS

"

I think the best thing you can do is to be aware that we are not indestructible, but use that awareness to live our lives as fully as we can. Be happy, love others, give service, and be awake!

"

MANY PEOPLE DIE AT TWENTY-FIVE AND AREN'T BURIED UNTIL THEY'RE SEVENTY-FIVE.

BENJAMIN FRANKLIN

"

"

IT IS NOT DEATH THAT A MAN SHOULD FEAR, BUT RATHER HE SHOULD FEAR NEVER BEGINNING TO LIVE.

MARCUS AURELIUS

"

GO ON MARCUS, TELL THEM HOW IT IS.

Yet again, we return to the waking sleep—alive but not aware, sleepwalking our way through life. If we truly feared the waking sleep, we wouldn't so easily fall into it. I don't want to lie on my deathbed and think, "Was that it?"

Back to Interface

I digress again. Things were going well. We were making solid progress with lean methodology and training. Over in Holland, they began to start the same journey, and Ton asked me to go over to support them. Their lean coordinator was a young Dutch woman. Again, a typical Dutch girl, blonde hair, blue-eyed. She was really nice and quietly spoken. I feared she would not have the personality to push the changes through. I listened to her lead a training session in Dutch: why am I here? Suddenly, in response to some derogatory comments, she shouted in English, "JUST FUCKING DO IT! This is an unofficial lean catchphrase. I knew then she would be fine.

I was using the Plan, Do, Check, Act (PDCA) method for problem-solving, as recommended in lean methodology, but there were some complex issues we could not solve. That's when I started looking into Six Sigma, an American methodology based on data and statistics.

Ton was a purist when it came to lean methodology, so I had to persuade him to let Emma and me train in Six Sigma. Eventually, he agreed.

We went to Leamington Spa to train at Smallpeice Enterprises (No, this is spelt correctly). Over a period of three months, we gained our Green Belts. We applied what we learned and managed to save over £100,000 in raw materials. I later progressed to Black Belt and Master Black Belt, and we sent up to 10 managers to train in Lean Sigma methodology. While NVQ 2/3 training was great for the shop floor, training managers in these advanced methodologies was always a smart move. These training sessions also brought you into contact with the best people in British Sugar, British Gas, BT, etc. Great benchmarking and best practice sharing.

One memorable evening, we were at the "Sizzling Sausage" pub in Leamington Spa. With us was a guy from Liverpool. It was the first time that day we met him, and it was the first time he had been in Leamington Spa. We were watching Liverpool on TV. This guy organised a betting game in the pub. People put money in to predict the score, and it was amazing to watch him work the room. Complete strangers talked to him and gave him money. He sat with us and had up to a hundred pounds on the table. The excitement in the pub was electric. At the end of the night, he paid out. When he left, the locals treated him like an old friend. He attended the course the next day, and then we never saw him again. I have always envied people who can communicate so effortlessly. Is it something about the Yorkshire personality, or is it a skill I lack?

I mentioned this to Karen, a marketing manager at Interface, while we were in a reception at work for something or other. She said let me show you. She took me by the arm and walked me around all the different groups of people. She smiled, made small talk, and introduced me to everyone; she was a natural. It frightened me to death.

Meeting people from other big companies often makes you question yourself. Are we as good as we think we are? We had consultants who promised the earth but, after visiting the site, said there was nothing they could improve. Are we missing something? How can we benchmark? We applied for the Best Manufacturing Awards. A company filmed a promotional video with Emma as the star. She loved it and did great. We were audited by Cranfield University and came second to Smith & Nephew, a bandage medical devices company. Basically, it's a clean room. Not bad for a company processing 40 tonnes of limestone a day! We had come a long way from the Industrial dispute.

I have heard other companies dismiss award applications as "gong chasing" or "self-indulgence," but I think it's more about their fear of not being as good as they think. We all want to be the captain of our ship. God forbid we might not be right. Better to go back to sleep.

The people on the shop floor took pride in showing visitors around on our open day to celebrate the site's success. Morale was high, and the workers felt proud of their achievements. The bonus scheme was paying out, and they were taking home more money in their pocket. Don't worry, the company was saving a significant amount on materials and labour.

Despite our success, the American owners were investing €6 million in a new Dutch bitumen line that could run twice as fast as ours in Shelf. I had been at Interface for five years, and altogether, I had spent 15 of my 31 years of work with the company. Steve once said, "If you cut me in half, I would have Interface running through my body. But I thought I could see the writing on the wall. I could not move up any further; the Dutch site was ramping up production, and we had already won national awards for efficiency and operations. Morale was good, and we were employing more people than when I first joined. It was time to go.

I was sad to leave the team, especially Emma, but there was nowhere left for me to go and much more to do.

I was contacted by a headhunting agency working for a printing company in the East Midlands called Bardon Box. During the interview, the General Manager let slip that he supported a certain football club from Salford. I immediately shut my notebook and said, "The interview is over." He looked shocked. The next few minutes were awkward as I explained I was a Leeds fan and I had a biased opinion against his club. I left. A couple of days later, they offered me the job.

Adventures in Football

Football has always been a big part of my life—God knows why. It's the true test for any philosopher.

> "ALL THAT I KNOW MOST SURELY ABOUT MORALITY AND OBLIGATIONS, I OWE TO FOOTBALL.
>
> ALBERT CAMUS"

The first game I remember watching was Leeds vs. Sunderland in the 1973 FA Cup final. We had a rental colour TV, the only one in the street, so our house was full of people—all Leeds fans. Leeds lost. I should have taken the hint.

Although my family showed little interest in football, we were generally Bradford Park Avenue supporters, coming from that side of Bradford. Park Avenue went bust. So, who to support? If anyone. Not many supporters went to support Bradford City, local rivalry and all that. I think most Avenue supporters went to the big team of the time—Leeds United.

My sister Mary was dating Phil, a Leeds fan from Wyke (and later her husband). As a birthday present, Phil took me to my first Leeds game at 15, I think in 1976. Leeds lost 1-3 to Aston Villa. Job done, I still couldn't take the hint, I was hooked.

Why? I don't know. Maybe it was the sense of belonging or the tribalism. For a few years, I was only a Leeds fan rather than a football fan. In later years, I've come to appreciate players like Messi and De Bruyne—who, in my opinion, are the best players I have ever seen, except, of course, for Eddie Gray, but in those days, I was a Leeds fan.

Once I started working, I could afford to attend away games. These were the bad old days when football hooliganism was at its peak.

I remember Coventry away, where approaching the ground, there was a new Housing estate where you could see a Leeds fan climbing up the flagpole to steal the Barrett Homes development flag. We were searched three times before getting into the ground. Leeds went 2-0 up, but Coventry equalised, and word spread that if Coventry scored again, we were invading the pitch.

Thankfully, they didn't, but outside the old Highfield Road ground, in the narrow-terraced streets, the police were keeping the rival supporters apart with truncheons and horses. I always found the West Midlands Police to be the worst. Leaving on the coach, we passed an ambulance with some police getting on the back. The Leeds fans chanted, "We'll see you all next year". One policeman just stuck two fingers up at us.

Another time, at Birmingham away in the cup, Leeds won, I think 2-1. I was standing at the back of the stand, and when Leeds scored, I jumped up and hit my head on a metal beam, cutting the top of my head. I always remember my now Brother-in-Law, Phil, calmly putting on his leather gloves, "Just in case," he said. As we left, a hill full of Birmingham fans started throwing stones at us. One hit me on the neck, causing a bloody scratch. Suddenly, the Leeds fans had had enough and charged up the hill, reminiscent of medieval battles; I followed Phil up the hill because I didn't know where else to go. Then the police arrived on motorbikes and horses, trying to keep everyone apart. I eventually made it back to the coach with a blood-stained scarf, looking like I was a wounded soldier from a war film.

Salford United away was another memorable one. The ball flew over Gordon McQueen's head, dropped at Brian Flynn's feet, and he put it in the net. Leeds won. I had taken the train to Manchester, and on the train groups of Leeds fans were roaming, looking for Salford fans. The taxi driver would only take us so far, and we had to walk the rest of the way, scarves hidden. We walked to the ground surrounded by enemy supporters. Eventually, we came to a group of supporters waiting to get on the ground with Leeds scarves, many of them bloodied.

Inside the stadium, it became clear that there were far more Leeds fans than expected (not all ticket game, pay on the door), so they started moving some Salford fans down the sides adjacent to the away end. They were not happy. Fighting everywhere. When we came out at the end of the game, as we came out we saw no enemy supporters. Safe then. As we were on the train, the police walked us down to the station in the centre of Manchester to the station, seemingly safe, until I saw a mass of Salford supporters in long black leather coats and the Salford scarfs bulging out at the top, heading our way. I was terrified, but the other Leeds supporters cheered and ran at them. Eventually, my friends and I got back on the train.

Hartlepool away in the cup was a strange one. The game had been postponed several times due to weather, so Phil could not come because of work. It was a night match, so I was on my own. Leeds won 6-2. They tried to keep the Leeds fans in at the end, but the doors were broken down, and we got out. Suddenly, I felt something and turned to see a bottle smash on the ground near me. A group of home supporters stood nearby. My first reaction was to run, but I turned straight into a big Leeds fan in a sheepskin coat and scarf. "Leeds don't run," he said. I turned back to see my attackers now being attacked by a group of Leeds fans. The big Leeds fan let me go, and I walked back to the coach.

Sheffield United away in the League Cup on a Tuesday night. Phil and I travelled with a group of Halifax Whites, who had decided, for reasons I still don't understand, to wear full gorilla masks. As we approached Bramall Lane, we were suddenly hit by a barrage of stones. We charged down the street, only to find out it was other Leeds fans throwing the stones. "Sorry lads, we thought you were Blades," they said.

After that, I stopped going to away games. They were just too eventful, and Phil and Mary were having kids, so he stopped going as well.

I once took my frog friends to a game at Elland Road. They came prepared with a bit of a picnic, including a bottle of diluted Ribena. Andy Rad and I smiled at their innocence and led them to stand in the Kop. Leeds scored, and as the crowd surged forward, Lida screamed. The picnic went flying, and the Ribena flowed down the terraces like blood. Lida later told me it was the most terrified she had ever been. Chris bought a scarf and later showed me photos of him wearing it in class, back at the school in Paris where he was teaching in.

The only time I was ever physically attacked was watching Halifax Town against Tranmere Rovers. I used to go to the Shay with my father-in-law. After the game, as we were walking past a group of supporters, one lad suddenly raised his hand and caught me on the chin before he and his mates ran off. Kids at The Shay. In all my football adventures, I never hit anyone, and I am happy about that.

I was there when Leeds won the last Division One title under Seargent. Wilko. It was, I think, a Sunday. My daughter Jade was born on a Friday, and within two hours of her birth, there was a Leeds scarf around her cot. Now, that's what you call a double whammy! After Jade was born, I stopped going to the games regularly to help raise her, especially after moving up to the Northeast.

Even though I did not have much money after splitting from my wife, I bought season tickets for both me and my daughter. She attended her first game when she was five—it was like a christening. I had to travel from Halifax to Newcastle to pick her up, then down to Leeds and then back to Newcastle to take her back home and then back to Halifax.

I continued to go to the finals. At the Championship play-off final in Cardiff, I witnessed what might be the worst job in the world. I was in a pub, full of drunken Leeds fans, all singing and dancing (this was before we lost 3-0 to Watford). The toilets were downstairs. You had to stand in a couple of centimetres of urine to get to the urinals. In there was a young guy trying to sell aftershave to Leeds fans—£1 a shot. I think I saw despair in his eyes.

Leeds was relegated from the Premier League and, went into administration twice, dropped into the third tier, and were owned by Ken Bates. I was there through it all.

At a play-off semi-final against Derby a few seasons ago, we were 1-0 up from the first leg, and 1-0 up in the first half before a calamitous misunderstanding between our centre-half and goalie let Derby back in. Leeds collapsed in the second half, and we lost. It was the worst I had ever felt after a game. I promised myself I'd never feel that bad again over football, and I haven't.

The Bielsa years brought joy and a sense of identity. I enjoyed every moment while it lasted, understanding that nothing lasts forever. Bielsa was sacked after a string of poor results, and the next season we were relegated again.

Why Football?

So why do I put myself through it? Well, it's all there, all life. Euphoria and sadness, hope and disappointment, loyalty and duty. You never know what will happen. Living with uncertainty. Friends and enemies. Tribal warfare, us and them, opinion and disagreement, joy and pain. It's being awake.

> "AND LIFE IS ITSELF BUT A GAME AT FOOTBALL.
>
> SIR WALTER SCOTT"

I remember a game against Blackpool on a cold November night a few years ago. Leeds was mid-table in the Championship and not doing well. It was freezing. There were only about 16,000 fans in attendance. Leeds won, but I still found myself asking: why bother? Duty or love. Duty is love.

“

I FELL IN LOVE WITH FOOTBALL AS I WAS LATER TO FALL IN LOVE WITH WOMEN: SUDDENLY, INEXPLICABLY, UNCRITICALLY, GIVING NO THOUGHT TO THE PAIN OR DISRUPTION IT WOULD BRING WITH IT.

NICK HORNBY, FEVER PITCH

”

I was recently watching an episode of the comedy *"Meet the Richardsons"*. Jon Richardson, the comedian, says in a moment of reflection, *"I love Leeds United, but Leeds do not love me."*

I think that is something we all feel—not just Leeds fans, but football fans everywhere.

Earlier in this book, I talked about how we need to have our heads in the clouds but our feet on the ground. This is what football is all about. Football, compared to consciousness, is pointless and nonsense. Everything compared to consciousness is nonsense. We need to remember that. But life is also meant to be experienced and enjoyed in all its highs and lows. Football is a great reminder of that—it wakes you up.

But it's still nonsense. Glorious, painful nonsense.

CHAPTER TWELVE

BENSON BOX AND THE NOTTINGHAM SCHOOL OF PHILOSOPHY

This was as big a change as moving to the Northeast. I was still paying maintenance for my daughter, and Janet's daughter had moved in with us while studying law at Wakefield College, later at Huddersfield University. This meant we couldn't sell up and move lock, stock, and barrel to the East Midlands. We would need two houses.

I lived in B&Bs and hotels for a few months while Janet would come down, and we would look for a cheap house to buy. With some of the money she obtained from her divorce and other bits of savings, we could just about scrape together a second mortgage.

The factory was in Bardon, and the nearest town was Coalville. Everyone warned us off living in Coalville, which was, as it sounded, an old pit town. All the pits were gone, but it was still seen as a bit rough. We looked around the area, but our finances limited our options.

One day, Janet called to say an estate agent had just told her about a house in Coalville that had come on the market that morning. We saw it at dinner time, made an offer, and it was done in 30 minutes. It suited our needs perfectly and was the right price. I lived there for three years and never had any trouble. I went down on Sunday Night and returned home Friday afternoon. It was emotionally hard for Janet and me to leave on a Sunday evening. Sometimes, it took me three hours to get home on Friday afternoon, so I was pretty tired. Football on Saturday or some other event, and then Sunday was spent preparing for the week ahead. Every few weeks, Janet would come down and clean the house, like someone cleaning out a rabbit hutch.

Benson Box produced printed cardboard packaging for the main supermarkets. It was a purpose-built factory, with printing, cutting, and gluing (finishing) and a hand-packing and window insertion department. It was lovely, with underground conveyors taking away the waste cardboard to an automatic baler, state-of-the-art equipment. Beautiful. All were built by the Benson family. The eldest Benson was retired, his eldest son, Andrew, was the Chairman, and his brother worked in Marketing. They also owned a company in Crewe specialising in medical packaging and another in Newcastle producing similar products to the Bardon site, which was the headquarters.

So, what did I know about printing? Nothing. Why did they want me? They thought they were already the best. Why did they want another Operations Manager from the same industry? They wanted someone who could add to their knowledge. Brave.

I was a bit concerned about my lack of technical knowledge, but as usual, I was up for the change and challenge.

My boss was the general manager and an accountant. His boss, Mark, the Managing Director, was also an accountant. They also had a Financial Director and a Finance Manager. I was the senior person in Operations. They were financially tightly controlled by Mark, who I think was a very good MD. He was brought in by Andrew to drive the company forward in terms of profit, and Mark did just that. The profit margins, I think, were the highest in the industry, but of course, they wanted more. I was responsible for Production, Quality, Warehousing, Engineering, Planning, and Transport (they had their own small fleet of trucks).

I built an office on the ground floor next to the factory and away from the office politics in the main upstairs offices. It was a 24-hour/6-day operation that went to 24/7 during the peak, which was the four months before Christmas. Out of 350 people, approximately 300 reported to me. To be fair, it was how I wanted it.

I began to implement lean tools such as OEE and 5S. Printing was still seen as an art form or craft industry. I changed the thinking from opinion to science, focusing on efficiency and numbers. Once, in the early days, the Print Manager was celebrating producing around 700,000 printed sheets in a day. We sat down and analysed the OEE, which was around 25%. In other words, what happened to the other 75% of the potential 2.1 million other sheets?

I sent most of the managers off-site to train in Green Belt. It was great to hear day-to-day conversations shifting to efficiency, numbers, and lean concepts instead of excuses, problems, and opinions. Factory efficiency, which was already good, improved. Profitability increased. I used my familiar tactic of training staff using grants obtained from Loughborough College. Many people achieved NVQs and management qualifications. Morale was good. It was nice not having to turn the company around – there was great energy on the site.

We applied to the "Best Manufacturer Awards" again and came second, this time to a food company in Merseyside. Bugger. However, we did win the award for Best Training Organisation. I had gone to London straight from home on the train, while the others went from Leicester. Afterwards, I went straight home with a smile on my face. The General Manager took the group around Ashby-de-la-Zouch for a session. It was not a good idea and was a taste of things to come. It's hard to be the boss and also a drinking partner.

I was asked to give a talk at the Global Manufacturing Forum at Cranfield University. I agreed. Just before the talk, the professor in charge tried to give me advice on what to say. He said, "Just tell the truth." I replied, "What is truth?" That shut him up.

Everything was going well. However, spending time away from home was hard. Thankfully, the School of Philosophy came to the rescue.

The Nottingham School of Philosophy

As soon as I moved down to Benson's, I joined the Nottingham school. I say "joined," but it was expected. In Leeds, I was in a high-level class called G Gents. It was male-only, with an average length of service of around twenty-five years. Since I was moving to the Midlands, it was assumed I would attend the much smaller Nottingham school.

Nottingham's senior group met on a Thursday at the home of the head of the Nottingham school, David. He was a millionaire, the MD of a building company, and had other businesses such as an undertaker's. He was tall, around fifty, and it was assumed he would one day take over the whole of the Northeast area. The group was mixed, with women and men, some long-term, but others new. If you had been in the school for 5-6 years, you were still classed as a newbie. It was about 30 miles from where I lived, but it often took an hour to get there due to traffic and only half an hour to get back.

I gave a lift every week to George, a refugee from the school in the North West. George was well over 60 and married for the third time to a much younger Chinese woman. He lived in the next town and was always decorating his house while his wife worked on developing hydrogen as an energy source. He was a good guy, but by Thursday, I was often done in, and on a few occasions, I nearly kicked him out on the motorway because of his constant talking. His history and career were amazing (he was an engineer who had worked all over the world, which is where he met Hun, his wife), and he had a good soul.

The philosophy classes were less rigid than those in Leeds because David was less strict. I was a bad student, often falling asleep during meditation and insisting we finish at 9.15 on the dot to allow me time to get home and to bed before the next day. If it went over, I would start putting on my coat to make sure David got the message. Do you think I'm passive-aggressive? Of course, David was very keen and often went over time.

There were some good people in the group, especially Alison, a good socialist (not many of those in the school) who had a great sense of humour, but was a little too politically correct for me, as we would discover later. I think they wanted George to be a tutor in the Nottingham school, but it was too far for him to come without transport, and he didn't want to do it. So, the last resort was me.

I was living on my own the week, and I needed a distraction, so I agreed. The classes were held at a solicitor's across from the park, where they held the annual Goose Fair. There were only two or three classes, and they were always being amalgamated due to lack of numbers. I was given the task of tutoring Part 1 with Alison as my assistant.

The group, as usual, followed the trend of being white, working and middle-class. It was a mixed group. I always went through all the reading material, which partly involved asking the students what they thought.

This is where my unfortunate sense of humour, quick responses, and lack of tact turned the sessions into fun. Well, I thought it was fun. Alison had an invisible red flag that she waved furiously whenever she thought I had overstepped the mark. Which was often. Students like Wendy and Paul remain friends to this day.

After a few weeks, one lady announced that she had read online that the school was a cult. I immediately said they should all leave. Stunned silence.

"Aren't you going to stop us?"

"No, it's a free country. I've been in the school for 15 years, and I don't believe it's a cult, but I'm not going to try and tell you it's not. You can work it out for yourselves."

The woman left, but her friends stayed. The laughter and fun continued, with real progression in terms of people feeling happier and calmer by applying the philosophical tools they learnt.

Why do people join these classes? Sometimes to try something new, to meet new people, or because they have a need. What they want is to learn while having some fun, and this group did. I treated them with respect and as equals in the search for knowledge. They treated me the same way. I made fun of them; they made fun of me. Usually, at least half of the Part 1 group would disappear in the first few weeks of the 10-week course when they realised it wasn't for them. In this group, very few left. Everyone got on well with each other, to such an extent that we decided to have our own Christmas night out in Nottingham.

We had a meal, then went out to a few pubs. As a good tutor, I left early (it's always better to do that as a manager as well). Afterwards, it went far too well. Some of the people never came back in the new year. There were talks of illicit photos and threats not to show them on social media where wives and husbands might see.

In term two, more people joined. Friends of people in term one joined their friends. The group grew to 12 or 13 strong. We talked about personal things, feelings that had never been touched on before. One man, a big builder, said his father had never told him he loved him. Silence. I said that if my father had told me he loved me, I would have called ChildLine. Silence, and then everyone burst out laughing, with Alison waving her imaginary flag.

Some of the group are still friends, and we keep in loose contact. Some got into meditation, and I was very proud that they trusted me enough to do it. The reputation grew in the school as a class that increased, not decreased. Once, a senior member of the school asked me what the secret was. I said, "We have fun."

Nanpanton

I was now living near Nanpanton, near Loughborough, where the school owned a country house on its own grounds, where we would meet for three weekends and one week a year.

I didn't like it.

They based the routine on an Indian ashram: up early for work at 6 a.m. and meditation at sunrise. Philosophical study and work filled the day, with a break after dinner and more study and work up until around 9 p.m., sometimes later. The work comprised either looking after the building and gardens or working in the kitchen. Breakfast, lunch, and dinner, with a few tea/coffee breaks, were all done by the students. Men and women were kept separate, even if you were married.

So why didn't I like it? The weekend was run by the school head. He gave most of the talks. There were other tutors, and senior members of the school who supported, issued out the work, organised the rooms, etc., but the head always took the classes.

It was very hierarchical. I am a Yorkshireman with socialist tendencies, so it did not suit me. I've always had a problem with authority. Someone needs to be in charge, and I get that. I do believe in the Philosopher King's idea. The head of the school was a Tory. He read the *Daily Telegraph*, had married a millionairess, and lived in a big house. His knowledge of Advaita and the Upanishads was unmatched in the school. However, other philosophical thoughts were not discussed. He would ask for opinions and then tell you what to think.

Whoever is in charge, you don't need to love them, definitely not fear them, but it would be good if you respected them. In all my business dealings, I have always disliked those who demand respect. Worse still are those who want to be loved.

I was once at a training awards ceremony in Huddersfield with a company where I was still relatively new. My old company was also represented. I noticed the two groups of students talking to each other. After the ceremony, back at work, I asked one of our people what they had been talking about. She told me they had been asking what I was like. They told them they would be fine and that I was fair but firm.

Being described as firm but fair is enough. In Yorkshire language, that makes me a kind of God.

At the Philosophy School, they took it too seriously. The head demanded respect; he was doing us a favour by being there. He was not humble; you were not there to enjoy yourself; you were there to be taught the error of your ways. Nanpanton was his dominion, and you were his servants—or at least that's how I felt. Others didn't feel that way and thought he was wonderful. It takes all sorts of vegetables to make a stew. I see myself as a large parsnip.

The message was always good when it came directly from the actual philosophy texts. Meditation and reflection were great for settling the mind. Advaita and consciousness are the way for me, but the delivery left a lot to be desired. Isn't it always the case that something good and spiritual gets spoiled when man tries to control it? Many people would disagree with my appraisal. Fine.

Anyway, when I began to get the students from my Nottingham class to attend, it got better. We had illicit drinking parties in the library late at night. Those were good times.

One of the things that used to annoy me was when, at break or dinner times, a senior tutor would ring a large brass bell to signal the end of the break. This was until someone hid the bell. I can now admit—it was me.

They were good people in the school, just trying to find a better way.

Back to Benson's

We won the Most Efficient Print Company in the Country award. Again, in London. No GM this time, but a good group of us from the factory went down. I did not feel great and left some of them drinking in the local bars. Unfortunately, I broke my dickie bow while getting dressed. I called one of the ladies to come and help. She was great, usually, but this time, she had a concerned look when I asked her to come to my room. I looked at her worried face and said, "I am not asking to shag you. I just need a hand fastening this bloody bow tie." She found a safety pin and saved the day. I later found out she was with someone else when I called. Not good. When it all came out, she asked for my help, and I gave it, but big cracks began to appear in what was otherwise a very good team. Does sex always get in the way?

A group of us went to Germany for the print exhibition, with some of the costs covered by our printing press supplier. At night, we explored the town. The supplier rep showed us around, and we had a good time. My favourite memory of that night was getting Jager bombs out of a side window of a bar. I downed it and turned around to see a man, naked except for a pair of red trunks and a cowboy hat, singing "She'll Be Coming Round the Mountain" or something like that. Germans can be fun. Who knew?

The second night took a turn for the worse. The GM was with us and got very drunk. He started following a hen party around the town, buying them champagne. The other guys asked me what we should do. I said, "Leave him," and walked away. We were staying on a barge converted into a hotel on the river. We all sat together for a nightcap when the GM turned up by himself, still drunk. He began talking, then crying. Two others started crying because he was crying. I said goodnight and left them to it. All I can say is that all three of them were supporters of that team from Salford.

The next morning, I was dreading what he would say. He came in with a smile on his face and said, "What was last night about?" Then he acted like nothing had happened. Not good.

At a board meeting, I gave the monthly figures on productivity, and the MD said, strangely, "Well, you don't need me; he's got it all working great." At the time, I thought it was a nice compliment, but a few months later, he had sold the business to private equity and moved to the South of France.

A new era began—transitioning from a family company to private equity. Mark had bought shares, but others, including the GM and myself, were not asked. The company changed. It had always been results-focused, but it became even more so. The private equity company brought in their own experts in sales, marketing, and operations. To be fair, they generally left me alone. They reviewed what I was doing and gave some good advice, particularly on sales and operational planning, but mostly left me to it. The GM, though, felt the pressure.

We hired a production manager to take some of the weight off my shoulders. The GM had sanctioned the recruitment, but the MD and another director disagreed, and after a few months, I had to let him go. I was not happy; it was not the production manager's fault; it was internal politics. Once, the GM came into my office, screaming that things needed to improve and that it wouldn't be him losing his job. However, he didn't tell me what I needed to improve.

The GM brought in a QC manager, reporting directly to him. We did not have major quality issues, but he thought that I should not be marking my own work. I warned him this could cause problems, and it did. The QC manager wanted to make her mark and complained about everything, mostly things that did not exist. It is a trait of incoming managers—they think everything before them was rubbish, and to thank heavens, they are there to save the company. It's a sign of insecurity.

This, along with the office affair causing issues within the team, the unstable nature of the GM, and the fact that I could take operations no further—efficiency was already up 30%—combined with my desire to go home, meant it was time to leave.

My leaving was good, held at an Italian restaurant in Coalville. Instead of the usual speech by the GM, the MD asked to say a few words. He thanked me and said I had brought facts and action to the company and that I was the best Ops Manager they had ever had. It was a nice gesture.

So, the company was doing well, despite the few issues I mentioned. I could have dealt with that, and the philosophy group was good. So why leave? Mainly, it was the desire to go home, but I think it is because I am still searching for something.

Plato's Cave

Here's a brief synopsis of what Plato discusses in *The Republic*:

The Allegory of the Cave is a Socratic dialogue recorded by the Greek philosopher Plato, a student of Socrates and one of the few people to write down his teachings, which were eventually compiled into books. The Republic is one such book, containing The Allegory of the Cave, a dialogue between Socrates and Plato's brother Glaucon.

In the allegory, Socrates imagines a group of people chained together inside an underground cave as prisoners. Behind the prisoners is a fire, and between them and the fire are moving puppets and real objects on a raised walkway. However, the prisoners are unable to see anything behind them, as they've been chained, stuck looking in one direction—at the cave wall—their entire lives.

As they look at the wall, they believe the shadows of objects cast by the moving figures are real things—and the only things. Their visible world is their whole world. The narrative goes on to imagine what would happen if one of the prisoners were forced to leave. What would they see? How would they adjust? Would they believe what they saw outside? What would happen to them if they returned to the cave? Would they still perceive things the same way?

The freed prisoner would likely return and try to liberate their fellow prisoners, now knowing how much more of the world exists outside the cave. However, Socrates and Glaucon agree that the other prisoners would likely kill the one who tried to free them, as they wouldn't want to leave the safety and comfort of their known world.

(Plato overview by MasterClass.com)

Since I first learned about Plato's cave in the School of Philosophy, it has always fascinated me. It makes me wonder if I am one of the people chained to a chair, watching unreal objects in silhouette, believing they are real. I don't think that's me.

So much of what I think and see happening is fantasy. I see people getting promoted and rising in businesses because they fit in better than others (sometimes, like me). They are safe in the sense that they won't rock the boat, but they also won't lead the organisation forward, restricted to one way of thinking—like people chained, watching shadows. I see myself as one of those who tries to escape, to see things as they truly are.

Once I've tasted freedom, I want everyone else to share in that freedom. So, I tell them.

In the allegory, this is when the people chained to the chairs try to kill me. Why? Because they don't want to know a different way. They're doing alright. Happy in their state and the status quo.

Here's my dilemma: I'm doing alright. Why do I need to search for something which may not even exist?

OK, if I escape and see reality for what it is—well done, me. So what? In a few hours, I'll be hungry. Bills will start coming in: electric, gas, mortgage—all the costs of modern life. Does being able to see things as they truly are pay the bills and put food on the table?

In the Advaita philosophy of the school, there is no duality. There is no difference between me as a conscious being and everything else as consciousness. But that does not work practically.

There are two levels. At the higher level, there is no difference between me and everything else head in the clouds. But on the other level, you have to exist in this society based on success, money, desire, and greed—feet on the ground. Maybe it's my council estate upbringing that drives my need to provide for myself and my nearest and dearest.

I often criticise myself for not becoming an MD or director more often than I did. I have the qualifications, I have the experience, but I don't have the personality. I find it hard to conform. This, I think, is my eternal conflict of head in the clouds and feet on the ground. I often get the balance wrong.

I could have stayed at many companies. In some situations, it might have worked out well, but I have always had an issue with authority. In most cases, those in power are the ones chained to the chairs, believing in a reality I think is nonsense. It's hard to work for those people. Certainly, with the GM at Benson's, it felt that way.

Am I going up my own arse? Is this an excuse for failures in my career? (It hasn't been that bad.) Probably.

CHAPTER THIRTEEN

ADVANCED SUPPLY CHAIN, LOVE AND SALTAIRE

I was contacted by an agency to apply for the post of Operations Manager at a company called Advanced Supply Chain in Halifax, which was 8 miles from where I lived. I went for an interview. The GM seemed ok but was rushed. The site was an old engineering company that had been converted into a clothes processing facility. It generally took boxed clothes from China, Taiwan, Vietnam, Bangladesh, etc., and the jumpers, dresses, and T-shirts were put on hangers, steamed, and organised into orders for customers like Asda, Next, Debenhams, and others.

After a quick first interview, I was invited to the second one with the Owner/MD. I had a quick walk around the site with the GM, and then the MD asked me what I thought.

I said it looked dirty, disorganised, and inefficient. The MD told me how he had built up the company from scratch with the Finance Director, and now it had a main office in Bradford, warehousing, and a large unit in Corby with an export department and freight business, including his own trucks. He did most of the talking. After a while, he said he would think about it and let me know the following week.

I knew he would offer me the job. The Halifax site had made losses for a few years on a £5m turnover. It was projected to make £50k profit for that year, largely due to the GM's efforts. The MD remarked that it was the sort of profit a good Fish and Chip shop would make.

The GM was a salesman who had worked his way up from the shop floor to GM. He pushed hard to achieve any profit. I thought he was a good salesman who worked hard.

I should not have taken the job.

By selling the house in Coalville, I could pay off my mortgage. By reducing my travelling and avoiding two sets of bills for rates, heating, and water, the lower wage was far offset by the savings, but I still should not have taken the job.

I should have waited for the right opportunity. I went from being a successful Operations Manager in the packaging industry, responsible for 300 skilled workers, to joining a dirty, minimum-wage, zero-hours company.

I knew I had made a mistake on my first day. I was introduced to the staff, and one of them was already the Operations Manager. I said to the GM, "I thought I was the Operations Manager."

"You are, but we haven't told him yet."

"What's going to happen to him?"

"We have not decided yet."

Great.

The workforce was made up mostly of Asians and Eastern Europeans, around 120 people. Nearly all were on zero-hour contracts. The conditions were so bad that questions had apparently been raised in Parliament by the local MP. It was dire.

There were no windows, and a thick grease coated the walls from when it had been an engineering company. People were searched every day before they left, in case they were hiding clothes.

There was a profit and loss meeting daily, where labour costs and volumes were compared to the cost/unit for the previous day, the current day, and the expected costs for the following day. If we were not going to make a profit, we would cut people by getting rid of any agency workers, forcing people to "bank" hours, not come in, and they had to pay the hours back when we were busier — with only 24 hours' notice.

For Asda, the biggest customer, we had to unload the boxes from the shipping container, palletise, store the pallets, take the clothes out of the boxes, and manually hang, steam, barcode, and separate them into storage hubs before loading them onto the trucks. We received £0.04/unit.

At any one time, there could be 500,000 units of clothing on site.

I soon got tired of being second to the incumbent Operations Manager.

There was a definite seasonality to the business. The run-up to Christmas was the busiest time, with Halloween fancy dress costumes, Christmas jumpers, etc. We needed to run two shifts. I volunteered to run the 6 a.m. to 2 p.m. shift.

I found a mouthy girl team leader, a real rough diamond with a heart of gold, who was always complaining but was very good at organising and talking to people, and an Asian team leader who knew the processes back to front. We had a line of 50 tables in one long row, split by a walkway in the middle. I put target boards on each side with an hourly target for the number of clothes hung. Each morning, we gathered the shift together, quickly went over what needed to be done, celebrated the best performer from the day before, cracked a few jokes, and got to work.

During the busy season, there were many temporary/agency workers. They were shown the best technique for processing clothes and checked every hour. Some walked out after an hour. Those who didn't meet the target after three hours were walked off the site in front of everyone as a warning.

Although we tried to make it as fun as possible — bars of chocolate for the best performers and small celebrations every time we broke a new record — it was brutal. I always think about it whenever I see shops selling cheap clothing. We outperformed the other shift, and everyone wanted to be on my shift.

I began cleaning the site, painting floors bright yellow, structures blue, and walls white. Yellow, blue, and white — hmm, it reminded me of a certain football club. There are factories from Newcastle to Leicester painted in these colours, and there had to be some advantages to being the boss.

The workers loved it, and so did the owners at Advanced (Leeds fans). We got them to "open up" new areas we had cleaned and repainted by cutting ribbons as if they were opening a new Town Hall. It did not cost much, but the effect on morale was huge.

Once the peak season finished, I was back on days. Still not the official Operations Manager, I was in a kind of no man's land. Nope, I wasn't going to settle for that. I looked to leave.

I applied to a textile mill in Leeds as a Production Manager. I had dealt with them in the past. After the first interview, they asked me to come in for a full-day interview, meeting the team, including the shop floor. When I arrived, I realised there were two other candidates in the same room. Well, this is different. I wasn't fazed; it seemed like fun.

I met the team — no problem. My knowledge of textiles was good, but what about the people on the shop floor? I was shown around the mill. It was dirty and needed a lot of work. You could tell at least ten generations of the same families had worked there.

I remember sitting in front of a group of Overlookers who were interviewing for their next boss. They asked me what I would change. I said, "No, you tell me what you would change." They were shocked. Then, I nodded at the appropriate times while they told me what was wrong.

That night, the Director and HR Manager called me and asked to meet at a local hotel, where they offered me the job. It was less money, and further to travel, but it seemed like a good way out of the situation at Advanced, so I accepted.

When I handed in my notice at Advanced, they were shocked. Why, I don't know. Surely, they understood why. The General Manager tried to talk me out of it, then the Owner. Still, I wasn't budging.

In a last-ditch meeting, they offered me the General Manager role. The current GM was moving to become the Group Sales Director, and I would have full autonomy over the site, with a pay rise of £10k more than the Leeds job.

General Manager, more money—I agreed and gave back word to the job in Leeds. I had only been with the company for six months and had gone from nearly being Operations Manager to General Manager. Now, it was all on me.

The staff at Holmfield were shocked, especially the Operations Manager, but some had already bought into a different style of management. We kept cleaning the place up, making it a better place to work. We still had our daily profit and loss meetings and weekly reviews with all employees on issues and profit. We still had high staff turnover, but we repainted the offices, cleaned the tables where the workers operated, and gave them anti-stress mats to stand on instead of the concrete floors.

I remember an old Asian gentleman saying thank you for that. He hardly spoke at all and knew very little English, but he said thank you. I felt humbled.

Morale improved, productivity improved, but we were still only making small profits.

We always had a nearby warehouse we rented before peak season to hold stock waiting to be processed. This year, we stacked the stock outside the building and covered it with tarpaulin to save costs. It worked, but it was difficult to keep the stock dry. Still, it saved money.

Then there were extras— this was where you made money. Storage, hangers, and extra processing were all charged for. We actively looked for anything we could charge.

Attached to the building were some fumigation rooms used to kill anything harmful. They were run by two guys from Liverpool who had developed a gas that killed mould, insects — anything. We checked garments for issues needing treatment. One year, we were processing Asda's schoolwear range, produced in Bangladesh, where insect control was poor. The clothes contained bugs and insects I had never seen before. We made good money treating hundreds of thousands of shirts, trousers, jackets, etc.

When someone found an insect in the clothes, they would run to the office delighted. We would send the evidence to Asda, who had no choice but to agree to the extra processing. Any shortcut was taken. It was the only way.

In my first full year, we made, I think, £150k. The second year, we made £550k on the same turnover that we had made £50k two years earlier. I had been lucky with the insects and had done some good work, but I still think that was my proudest achievement. Funny — I've won big awards at Interface and Benson's, had my name in magazines, and been lauded at large functions, but it was at Advanced that I made the most difference. I kept 120 people employed in difficult circumstances, made their lives easier, gave them some fun, and made some money.

It was hard.

I cleared cardboard boxes from conveyor belts, sacked people, and faced tough daily P&L meetings. It was taking a toll on me.

Back to Leeds Philosophy School

As I had returned home, it was back to my old group, with the same tutor. It had been three years, but it felt like a week. The rest of the group were all long-timers and older than me. I think they took it all too seriously.

Once, a member of the group said that he had seen consciousness while eating his rhubarb crumble with cream. There was silence. I said, "That was ridiculous"!

"You have custard with rhubarb crumble, not cream". They just looked at me. I wonder if they had missed me.

Once, while Janet and I were walking through some woods, we came across a magpie that was trapped in a box. I released it. In the meeting, I said I had seen the absolute in the freedom of the magpie. The tutor said I was not advanced enough to see the absolute; only the head of the school was. Hmm. I still enjoyed the meditation and the reminders of what was important and what was the play. There was nothing much new.

The school decided that, to boost numbers, they would give the first term free. I was chosen to tutor the first group. It worked because we had over 20 people on the first night. You always get a few people leaving, but by the end of the 10-week course, we still had around 15 people attending. This group was different. A different dynamic with some upper working/middle class, but there were also some who could never afford the £70 joining fee. It challenged me because the questions were different. They were based on a need to understand not just philosophy but also their place in the world. Some walked for hours to attend the class because they couldn't afford the bus. At the end, out of 15 people, only 2 or 3 paid to move to term 2. I tried to get the school to provide for the obvious need, but to no avail. There are a few millionaires in the hierarchy; I don't think they got it. This book is for them, besides my egotistical self.

I had 2 assistants; one was my stepdaughter, and the other a lady called Surinder. One of the students kept badgering Surinder to tell her where she was from. Eventually, Surinder told them "Dudley".

The next term, I was sent to start my first term in Saltaire, on the other side of Bradford. The group was the usual mix of old and young, white, working and middle class, some wanting a night out, some looking for something deeper. The term went well, as did the second and third. We had fun, and you could see the class progressing in happiness and understanding. There were two sisters, some nurses and other managers, a retired couple, good people.

We got to the time when I was being pushed to get them to Nanpanton for a weekend. I had my reservations but followed instructions, and around five of them came on the weekend with other newbies from around the branches. Disaster. It was run by a tutor who was after the top job. The theme was devotion. Devotion!!!

What should have been a relaxed introduction to retreats and meeting others of a like mind became an exercise in philosophical discipline based on the Indian ashrams' focus on obeying and following directions. The two sisters left after the first night. My wife had brought newbies from her class in Brighouse. She came to me with the material given to her by the head tutor to give to a large group. I read it, screwed it up, and threw it on the fire. I took both groups, and we discussed why they were there and what they wanted to get out of philosophy. A few laughs, a few philosophical principles, and job done. After three terms (a year), my class lasted another two weeks following the feedback to the others from those who attended. "But you are so free," said one of the sisters. "That was like prison." They were right.

Adventures in Love and Devotion

"

ONE WORD FREES US OF ALL THE WEIGHT AND PAIN IN LIFE. THAT WORD IS LOVE.

SOCRATES, GREEK PHILOSOPHER

"

I've been avoiding this. Having been blessed with ugliness, I have never had to fight women off; quite the opposite. Is that what love is? A physical attraction? I hope not. I can usually make women laugh, and I hope

I'm interesting. I think love is more than just physical—more important, vitally important.

Let's start with Socrates' version of love, as told by Plato. Socrates/Plato stated there are 3 kinds of love:

> “
>
> EROS IS HELD TO BE A COMMON DESIRE THAT SEEKS TRANSCENDENTAL BEAUTY—THE PARTICULAR BEAUTY OF AN INDIVIDUAL REMINDS US OF TRUE BEAUTY THAT EXISTS IN THE WORLD OF FORMS OR IDEAS.
>
> PHILOSOPHY OF LOVE – INTERNET ENCYCLOPEDIA
>
> ”

So this does incorporate sex and desire but also the beauty of ideas. The Sanskrit word for nature is "Prakriti." It is natural for men and women (or any of the varied genders now available) to feel desire for whichever particular gender takes their fancy. If not, the world would soon come to a juddering halt. It's in our Prakriti. Sex is natural. Love is natural. Love is **Love**.

SONNET 116: LET ME NOT TO THE MARRIAGE OF TRUE MINDS

“

LET ME NOT TO THE MARRIAGE OF TRUE MINDS
ADMIT IMPEDIMENTS; LOVE IS NOT LOVE
WHICH ALTERS WHEN IT ALTERATION FINDS,
OR BENDS WITH THE REMOVER TO REMOVE.
O NO, IT IS AN EVER-FIXÈD MARK
THAT LOOKS ON TEMPESTS AND IS NEVER SHAKEN;
IT IS THE STAR TO EVERY WAND'RING BARK
WHOSE WORTH'S UNKNOWN, ALTHOUGH HIS HEIGHT BE TAKEN.
LOVE'S NOT TIME'S FOOL, THOUGH ROSY LIPS AND CHEEKS
WITHIN HIS BENDING SICKLE'S COMPASS COME.
LOVE ALTERS NOT WITH HIS BRIEF HOURS AND WEEKS,
BUT BEARS IT OUT EVEN TO THE EDGE OF DOOM:
IF THIS BE ERROR AND UPON ME PROVED,
I NEVER WRIT, NOR NO MAN EVER LOVED.

WILLIAM SHAKESPEARE (POETRY FOUNDATION)

”

I am happily married. Not sure the wife is. This sonnet describes how I see my relationship with her. Age does not change my opinion or the delight I feel every time I see her. When we have impediments, we admit them. I'm far from perfect; why should she be? She is the star to my wandering ship.

> “
>
> BEING DEEPLY LOVED BY SOMEONE GIVES YOU STRENGTH, WHILE LOVING SOMEONE DEEPLY GIVES YOU COURAGE.
>
> LAO TZU,
> CHINESE PHILOSOPHER
>
> ”

But what about the beauty of ideas? This is where I think we are losing out. Where is the appreciation for the beauty of ideas today? Have we become so cynical that we can no longer see the beauty in art, music, nature, the written word, or even a perfect pass in football or a beautiful philosophy?

As I have said, I still cry at sad movies or when, "surprise, surprise," the people who at first disliked each other now, after adversity, fall in love. A beautiful sunrise, a beautiful sonnet by Shakespeare—these moments move me.

Has life become so hard? Are our opinions so fixed? Is our cynicism so strong that we do not trust ourselves to give in to beauty or love?

In part one of the Philosophy course, there's a week dedicated to beauty. It's something we all can feel, but the subject of that feeling of beauty is often different for each of us. That feeling of love and beauty, though, is the same for us all. It's universal.

It's causal, something all humankind can feel. Have we forgotten that feeling, like some ancient wisdom lost to us? The world is full of beauty—wake up and enjoy it.

The beauty of ideas is under threat. As discussed earlier, it's hard to find the truth in things, so we stop looking. There are some great ideas and thoughts from both the ancient and modern thinkers—we just have to look, listen, and evaluate without prejudice. Easier said than done.

> “PHILIA, IN CONTRAST TO THE DESIRING AND PASSIONATE YEARNING OF EROS, ENTAILS A FONDNESS AND APPRECIATION OF THE OTHER.
>
> PHILOSOPHY OF LOVE – INTERNET ENCYCLOPEDIA”

This relates to friends and family. That close bond we feel with our mother, father, siblings, besties, and mates. So many families now are estranged, mine included in some ways. Disagreements, feelings of not being valued, others being seen as favourites—it's all nonsense.

I am one of six. Second to last. Second favourite brother out of two. I don't care. My family is my family. We're bonded by blood. My brother likes the Nolan Sisters, and I like AC/DC. I don't care. We see each other rarely now—christenings and, more frequently, funerals. It doesn't matter. They are still my family. Life is too short for falling out. What good does it do? Enjoy your family, accept them for who they are, and treasure your shared heritage.

I think I have been lucky with friends. I've certainly had times when friends were hard to find. Or times when I could not find time to see all my friends. Some friends have stayed with me for years, some have come and gone. I'm grateful to them all. Men are not great at keeping in touch—this is life. Make friends, enjoy their company, and live. Understand the stages of life everyone goes through. I love them all.

> AGAPE REFERS TO THE PATERNAL LOVE OF GOD FOR MAN, AND OF MAN FOR GOD, BUT IT IS EXTENDED TO INCLUDE A BROTHERLY LOVE FOR ALL HUMANITY.
>
> PHILOSOPHY OF LOVE – INTERNET ENCYCLOPEDIA

God, don't get me started. Please replace "God" with anything you hold dear—even God! From my undoubtedly limited knowledge of religions, none say go out and kill someone for their beliefs if they are different from yours. It's mankind that's the problem, not religion, philosophy, or any other idea. It's mankind. It's those trying to twist religion or philosophy for their own gain or power. The Second World War was fought against fascism because fascism sought to subjugate one race of people to another. This is a righteous war. Sometimes, it is our duty (and duty is love) to protect those who would be harmed by false prophets or lies. Why? Because we should love one another and treat each other with respect. Everyone has the right to live as they wish, as long as it doesn't harm or impoverish others. You may not like what I have to say, but I hope you will allow me the right to say it. Black, Brown, Yellow, or White—I don't care. Everybody wants the same thing: to be happy and fulfilled. It's back to Maslow.

So, love your fellow man. He's probably trying to get by just like everyone else. But fight against those who would take your, or others', freedom away.

"

WHERE THERE IS LOVE THERE IS LIFE.

MAHATMA GANDHI,
INDIAN ACTIVIST

"

“

WHEN YOU ARISE IN THE MORNING, THINK OF WHAT A PRIVILEGE IT IS TO BE ALIVE, TO THINK, TO ENJOY, TO LOVE...

MARCUS AURELIUS, ROMAN EMPEROR & PHILOSOPHER

”

CHAPTER FOURTEEN

HOWDENS AND THE LAST HURRAH AT THE PHILOSOPHY SCHOOL

I was not particularly looking to leave Advanced, but I was approached by an agency to apply for a job at Howdens Joinery, based, obviously, at Howden in East Yorkshire, as a Factory Manager. I went for the interview with the Production Director, HR Manager, and a miserable Engineering Manager who sat in the corner giving me the dead eye.

At the interview, I described my experience as usual. But what was interesting was their company culture. They really looked after their people, and I mean in a way that was different from any other company I had seen. Bonuses, Christmas parties costing up to £750k, events in London on Park Lane, bowling competitions, tickets to Wimbledon, Six Nations Rugby, children's Christmas parties, Easter eggs—you name it, they did it. Annual share dividends and bonuses, which are paid out in full. I left saying that even if I didn't get the job, I applauded them for what they were doing. In the end, I didn't get the job, which was fair enough.

A few weeks later, they phoned the agency back, telling them they had another job for me. I went for another interview, but this time as a Continuous Improvement Sustainability Manager at a higher grade than the previous role. I met the head of Project Management and Engineering—or something like that. He was called Roy and was a Geordie from Nissan in his late 50s, going bald, with a bit of a goatee beard. He always wore a tight white shirt and thought he was God's gift to women. It turned out that most of the senior management were Geordies who had once worked for Nissan. The meeting went well, and I was invited to another interview with the Director of Engineering and Manufacturing. The receptionist told me I was now meeting the man in charge. I always talk to receptionists; generally, they know what's going on and who's who. This didn't work in one company in Oldham, though, where the receptionist had a photograph of her two young sons wearing Salford United shirts. I joked that it was child abuse and that I was going to report her to child services. She didn't appreciate the joke.

The meeting went fine, and they said they'd think about it. He told me they had their first-ever CI manager a year ago, who told them they were rubbish in terms of lean manufacturing and that everything needed to change. They sacked him. It's worth mentioning that Howdens was only 25 years old at the time, having risen from the ashes of the old MFI group. In 25 years, it had grown from nothing to £1.2 billion in sales (closing in on £2 billion now) with over 300+ depots at the time, selling to trade only, and with very impressive profits. It was created by an ex MFI sales director, I think, who had the vision to move away from big, costly showrooms that supplied the public, to become a specialist kitchen supplier for the trade. More about him later.

Weeks passed, and Roy was ill. Eventually, I was invited to an expensive dinner at The Grand Hotel in York. Roy was there with a very expensive consultant. We chatted about everything except the job. Then, when the consultant went to the loo, Roy leaned over and said, "Do you still want the job?"

"Yes," I said.

"I will send you the paperwork tomorrow."

We finished the meal, and the next day, the offer came over in an email.

I handed in my notice at Advanced. They countered with an offer of a directorship in charge of continuous improvement—but I'd had enough. They had the last laugh by withholding my bonus.

The last Christmas party with Advanced was as eventful as usual people taking drugs in the toilet, people peeing in the plant pots, and being asked to leave the premises early by the owners or the police would be called. We all piled into the local bars in Halifax after that. The two owners were good to me, saying that if I ever wanted to come back, I could.

I started at Howdens on the 2nd of January—not a great day to start. I was put in an open-plan office (hadn't been in one of those for a long time) with some Factory Managers, Planning, and Engineering, including the miserable one from the interview. After a bit of moving around, I sat next to the window in a group of four with Neil, a Factory Manager, Mike (the miserable engineer), and his secretary. This was a world away from the day-to-day stress I was used to. No one reported to me, I was on more money, but they didn't really know what to do with me. There was a small team of CI people in an office in one of the nine "factories" on-site who reported to the Planning Manager. Aware that the previous person in my role had been sacked, I just relaxed and waited to see what would happen.

Bit by bit, I began getting on with the small group at the table, mainly by talking philosophy and taking the mickey out of everyone. One day, I was talking to Mike's engineering secretary, who was very open to a laugh. I told her that she and I could never get together. When she asked why, I said I had standards and wouldn't lower them. Mike and Neil were initially shocked at what I said, but then they realised I was taking the mickey out of myself, not the secretary, and soon began laughing. Howdens was a prim and proper company—no one had talked like this before. I was the highest management grade in the room. This wasn't how things were usually done. The secretary, who was quite attractive, acted shocked, but she took it in the spirit it was intended and began to laugh. Just to note, I am blessed with ugliness.

Mike, Neil, and I met for lunch and afternoon tea nearly every day. I have worked with many people in my career and had some great teams, but the friendship we created together was the best I ever had. Mike, the miserable engineer, and Neil, the factory manager, are now some of my closest friends. They helped me enormously in getting through those years at Howdens. We watched each other's backs in a company rife with office politics. All of us have had our dramas in life, and we have always been there for each other. I am blessed. Even though we have all now left Howdens, we still meet every three months at Mike's holiday cottage in the North Yorkshire Moors and get drunk at the local pub.

The problem was that the original CI manager, the one they sacked, was right. The company was inefficient in terms of operational performance, 5S, and lean principles. The founder had got it right with his strategy of dealing with the trade, not consumers. Howdens built carcases, worktops, and trims at the Howden factory using modern machinery while buying the rest from abroad. He set up depots with a model that encouraged more purchases through discounts: the more you bought, the more you saved. Everything was kept in stock, so there was never a shortage. Joiners who installed kitchens loved this system. Customers would go through their chosen joiner, who showed them the glossy Howden brochure. Once they picked their kitchen, Howdens designed it and provided a quote with discounts, and the customers thought they were getting good value. No waiting for stock, good quality products, and favourable credit terms meant profit margins were great for both the joiner and Howdens. The growth was fantastic. Employing engineers/managers from Nissan in the northeast to set up a factory, which was never truly efficient, but was able to build stock through the year to ensure they never run out of stock during the vital October / November period where everyone decides they want a new kitchen for Christmas.

But after years of success, increased turnover, full bonuses, and great profits, the company got lazy. They thought they were impregnable, and the original team from Nissan now thought they were gods. I was once asked to create a Value Stream Map based on projected growth. I did, highlighting areas that could face challenges in the future. I identified a few departments that needed attention, especially the warehouse, which I predicted would struggle to meet future demand. I added little explosions to show where the bottlenecks would be. The head of Engineering and Manufacturing was furious—who was I, after only a few months at the company, to tell him and his team they had missed something?

During the next busy October-November period, as I had predicted, the warehouse couldn't handle the demand, and the manager was dismissed. I rebooted and trained teams in 5S. I delivered yellow belt training sent people off to train for Six Sigma green belts, and the improvements rolled out steadily. However, you couldn't discuss your past experiences at other companies—nothing was supposed to be better than Howdens. It was hard to argue, given the company's profits. Regular updates were given on how well the company was doing and how fortunate we were to have such management.

Every now and then, you were invited to a curry night with the founder. You had to wear a tie, and the food was always preordered to his preferences. The entire restaurant would be booked for Howdens staff. You couldn't start eating until he did, nor could you excuse yourself to go to the toilet while he gave his update. Questions were welcome, but anyone who asked the wrong one could be passed over for promotion. No one could leave until he left.

On the other hand, Howdens did go out of their way for staff. Once, I was responsible for taking a team of ten-pin bowlers to Skipton. As we got on the coach, the Senior Manufacturing Manager told me to "look after the team," meaning no expense was to be spared. We stopped at the venue the day before the competition, practised, and drank for five hours. We stayed at the Coniston Cold Hotel for two nights. The rule was that everyone had to be in bed before midnight. At 11:55, we were the last ones in the bar, except for senior management. I dutifully sent the team—and myself—to bed. We didn't win the competition against the different sales, factories, or warehouse teams, but everyone still got a bottle of spirits from me as a runner-up prize.

The second night, during the presentation evening, the team from Runcorn went to the bar early to watch Liverpool playing in Europe. Senior management was furious, and the team was disciplined by their site manager when they returned to the factory. Rules—so many unwritten rules.

I think I progressed. I got involved in projects, automation and worked with engineering consultants to begin introducing robots to the processes.

Once a year, at budget time, they gathered the senior operations management team to discuss cost-cutting. "If you cannot save £250k, leave your company car keys on the table and leave," they would say—more bravado. Luckily, I didn't have a company car. Of course, no one handed in their car keys. At one meeting, they discussed cutting staff costs. That's when I got a new boss, the Head of Engineering. As we sat down, he casually mentioned that since I was the newest person in his department, he had included me in the cost-cutting plan. But, he assured me, it would never actually happen. I wasn't happy about it, but I recognised his right to explore cost savings if necessary. While my name wasn't mentioned, my job title was. In that meeting were managers both above and below me. The meeting was chaired by someone angling to replace the Geordie, the soon-to-retire President of Operations, or something like that. He was a Mackem, and I never thought he was particularly good at his job. He certainly looked the part, but if he was skilled in anything, it was politically manoeuvring his way to the top. As usual, the meeting concluded without any solid outcomes—it was just another fishing expedition.

However, this Mackem then sent the individual reports to everyone who had attended the meeting, essentially revealing what I earned and how much it would cost to let me go. This was not right.

PRINCIPLE TEN

“

ONE SHOULD NEVER BE AGITATED UNDER ANY CIRCUMSTANCES. THERE MAY BE OCCASIONS WHEN A HARD LINE IS NECESSARY, USUALLY FOR THE SAKE OF EDUCATION, BUT TAKING A HARD LINE IS NOT NECESSARILY GETTING AGITATED. ONE CAN TELL THE DIFFERENCE BETWEEN RIGHTEOUS AGITATION OR WRONG AGITATION. IF ONE IS WRONGLY AGITATED, ONE CANNOT TAKE RIGHT ACTION, SO THIS HAS TO BE AVOIDED.

SHRI SANTANANDA SARASWATI, GOOD COMPANY 1987, THE STUDY SOCIETY

”

I tried not to get agitated, but I probably did because this was wrong and careless. Ignoring it would have been better, but that is not my way. I sent him an email, complaining that he was sharing my personal details with people who had no right to know them, which wasn't right. The next week, he asked to see me. He said he was unhappy about the tone of my email. I was disgusted. I told my boss about it, who then told the Mackem's boss, and eventually, the Mackem was informed that he was out of line. He never apologised—he was heading for the top. And he got there.

Despite its cultural issues, I liked Howdens. Mike and Neil were great; the pay was good, and the work was steady. But the 106-mile round trip every day... the idea was for Janet and me to move to East Yorkshire, but we couldn't find a house better than the one we had without taking on a huge mortgage. It was also a long commute for Janet to maintain her yoga classes. Driving two to three hours a day was wearing me down. I started to develop repetitive strain injuries in my calf from constantly pressing the accelerator.

One Friday night, Janet and I were in a local pub, and the owner of Advanced was there. He was delighted to see me. Since I had left two and a half years earlier, the site I had managed had lost significant amounts of money. He begged me to return. I said he couldn't afford me. He replied that he would match anything Howdens was paying. It was nice to feel like a big fish in a small pond again—to be wanted. It played to my ego.

I sent him my financial details. He arranged for me to meet his Operations Director at a local hotel. The director had just come back from a losing argument with the owner and the Sales Director. He seemed subdued and was looking to me for support against people I had known for years. He appeared weak. My return to Advanced seemed like a done deal.

I met the owner again one Saturday afternoon. He admitted he'd been drunk when we had met a month earlier. Here was the big hint—he wasn't sure about hiring me anymore. But I didn't take the hint. I never do. This was my chance to realise I was making a mistake, but I didn't take it. I had agreed to return to the Holmfield site with total control over P&L and all functions—to be a kind of god. All I had to do was make money.

I handed in my notice at Howdens. I had to give six months' notice, but they let me go after five. My boss told me I could change my mind up until my last day. Another hint I didn't take.

I wasn't living in the present. I was living in a fantasy. I have no patience.

"

HAVING CONFIDENCE AND PATIENCE. IF THERE IS NO CONFIDENCE, THERE CAN'T BE PATIENCE. THESE TWO ARE UNITED. SO SANATAN DHARMA WANTS INDIVIDUALS TO DEVELOP CONFIDENCE AND PATIENCE.

SHRI SANTANANDA SARASWATI, GOOD COMPANY 1987, THE STUDY SOCIETY

"

Adventures Living in the Present

We have talked before about Nurse Imagination, for those living in a fantasy and waking sleep, tending to people who believe that nothing will ever change.

Nurse Imagination conveniently forgot all the reasons why I left Advanced in the first place: the daily P&L reports, the constant pressure to meet production targets, and scraping every penny from the customers. In my imagination, I was returning as a hero—the person who had once turned the site around and would do so again. I was escaping the lack of respect and kudos at Howdens for the hero worship at Advanced.

I wasn't thinking; I was just hoping and looking for an escape. I wanted to be a big fish again, to be back in charge. I needed my ego boosted.

What was the alternative? Living in the present, seeing things as they truly are. Understanding your own feelings, knowing yourself, having patience, and creating a plan that benefits both yourself and others. Yet, after years of philosophy, I still wasn't getting it right. I believe that if you don't learn your lessons, they will be repeated—and moving back to Advanced was a perfect example.

> TO LIVE IN THE PRESENT MOMENT IS A MIRACLE. THE MIRACLE IS NOT TO WALK ON WATER. THE MIRACLE IS TO WALK ON THE GREEN EARTH IN THE PRESENT MOMENT, TO APPRECIATE THE PEACE AND BEAUTY THAT IS AVAILABLE NOW.
>
> NHAT HAHN, AZ QUOTES

So, how do you get into the present moment, and how do you stay there?

Is it the natural state of man to be asleep? Is the true challenge of life to escape from that waking sleep and come into the present, like stepping into the light from Plato's cave or achieving Maslow's self-realisation?

We have talked about waking sleep before. When you spend all your time thinking about the past—usually wrongly because your current feelings taint those memories—or thinking about the future—usually wrongly because we project our current positive or negative thoughts onto it. Drifting from one day to the next, riding the highs and lows of daily life with little control over either, or living in a fantasy where we are always the star—this is waking sleep.

We spend most of our lives here.

Then, at the end of life, we wonder, "What was that all about?"

"

I REACHED THE PINNACLE OF SUCCESS IN THE BUSINESS WORLD.
IN OTHERS' EYES, MY LIFE IS THE EPITOME OF SUCCESS.
HOWEVER, BEYOND WORK, I FOUND LITTLE JOY.

IN THE END, WEALTH IS JUST A FACT OF LIFE I HAD GROWN USED TO.
AT THIS MOMENT, LYING ON MY SICKBED AND REFLECTING ON MY LIFE, I REALISE THAT ALL THE RECOGNITION AND WEALTH I ONCE TOOK SUCH PRIDE IN HAVE FADED AND BECOME MEANINGLESS IN THE FACE OF DEATH.

ALLEGEDLY, THE LAST WORDS OF STEVE JOBS, BILLIONAIRE, WHO DIED AT 57.

"

I hope my last thoughts are more like,

> "IT'S BEEN A GOOD KNOCK."
>
> RON FROM THE THURSDAY MURDER CLUB, SO RELAXED AFTER HIS FIRST MASSAGE THAT HE THOUGHT HE WAS DEAD. RICHARD OSMAN, 2023

Not being in the present, being in a waking sleep, means we miss all the potential of now, including seeing things as they truly are.

This is the real influence on our future because being awake helps us make decisions based on the truth of the moment.

Waking sleep triggers automatic responses to situations, so we don't need to think. Have you ever arrived somewhere and wondered how you got there? Or entered a room and forgotten why you went in?

And then there's Nurse Imagination.

If you do ever wake up, don't worry—Nurse Imagination will be right there to put you back to sleep. Your mind will start to wander—What's for tea? When to book that next holiday? Or dreaming of glory and escape from your current situation.

Ask yourself: How much time do you spend in waking sleep?

Can we only see the truth when we are awake? Yes.

Can we see the truth when we are in waking sleep? No.

> WHAT'S WRONG WITH LIVING IN A DREAM WORLD? YOU HAVE TO WAKE UP!
>
> SUE MONK KIDD QUOTE FANCY

Some people never wake up, and why should they? Be asleep, be happy—but be aware that by not learning your lessons, you're missing something important. Not with fear, but with a clear view of what's really happening.

Can you always live in the present? My old philosophy tutor in the SES said that being truly awake for 30 minutes would feel like a lifetime.

Agreed—but I also think we need some waking sleep. To give your brain a rest. I enjoy switching off to watch football or reading a book.

So, what's the difference between watching football and living in the present?

Choice.

I choose to switch off and watch the footy. Then, I try to choose to live in the present. I'm not looking for answers when I watch sports—I'm just enjoying the match.

Is this easy to do? No.

It takes practice, and most of the time, I still fall back into waking sleep.

But... every now and then, I achieve awakening, and it's joyous.

How do I achieve that?

By understanding that the present moment exists.

By gaining knowledge from philosophy that has stood the test of time.

By listening to the wise, whose advice is not tainted by self-interest or grand ambition.

By putting what I've learned into practice and learning from the outcomes.

And, of course, through meditation.

> "MEDITATION IS WHAT MAKES AN INDIVIDUAL STEADY, PEACEFUL, AND CAPABLE, BECAUSE THROUGH IT, HE FINDS HIS WAY TO THE SELF, WHICH IS LIMITLESS AND HOLDS ALL THE TREASURES THE WORLD IS AWARE OF.
>
> SHRI SHANTANANDA SARASWATI"

So why is this important? Because it's a choice that most people don't realise they have. They can stay chained to the chair in Plato's cave or remain at the base levels of Maslow's hierarchy—or they can choose not to.

> “
>
> IF YOU ARE DEPRESSED, YOU ARE LIVING IN THE PAST. IF YOU ARE ANXIOUS, YOU ARE LIVING IN THE FUTURE. IF YOU ARE AT PEACE, YOU ARE LIVING IN THE PRESENT.
>
> LAO TZU, FEARLESS SOUL
>
> ”

To make that choice, you first have to understand that you have a choice.

The School of Philosophy—It's time to go. The principle of giving back is right. You receive, you benefit, you pass it on. Maybe even better—just give? The School of Philosophy is rightly based on this. I was teaching in Leeds on Wednesdays, attending my group on Thursdays, and going to Nanpanton for one full week and three weekends a year. For me, teaching a group on Wednesdays was the most beneficial experience. Other people's doubts and questions really make you assess your own thoughts and challenge what you're trying to convey.

The class I was attending was mostly for me to remember the philosophy and meditation. It was very useful, but after 20 years, it was more about reinforcing what I already knew rather than learning anything new.

Janet was essentially running the Brighouse branch—teaching, supporting, and organising the 2–3 classes. Glaive was the nominal head because he was in a higher group, and although Janet didn't mind, as Glaive was a great guy, it wasn't right.

At Nanpanton, they always asked Janet to take charge of the kitchen. Janet had run the kitchen for years, doing her best to create good meals from basic vegetarian ingredients. But running the kitchen meant that Janet never stopped and was exhausted after a week. She wanted someone else to take over, but they kept insisting she do it. We missed one weekend because Janet's daughter was getting married in Italy. Her tutor asked Janet if her daughter knew that being part of the school meant she should plan her wedding around school activities. Someone had lost the plot.

One weekend at Nanpanton, the head of the North East told the attendees—including Janet and me—that he was confident he could go to the head of the school and say that we were all now devotees of the school.

I struggle with being a devotee of anything. As can be seen from this book, I have a problem with authority. I listen, evaluate, and if the ideas are better than mine, I adopt them. I cannot follow blindly. The closest I get to devotion is with Leeds United—and that has been a disaster.

Janet decided to leave the school after being a member for twenty years. She told her tutor, who challenged her to tell the others. At tea break, she called everyone to attention, told them she was leaving, and wished them all good luck. I was so proud of her. I stayed another year, mainly because I was tutoring a great group of people and didn't want to let them down. The group became too small to continue, and I left.

I definitely want to give thanks for everything the school taught me. My current philosophy on life is largely based on the teachings of the school. The teachings are right—the organisation...

CHAPTER FIFTEEN

BACK TO ADVANCED

First day back at the head office in Bradford, I was warmly welcomed by the owner. He was delighted to show me the progress the company had made over the two and a half years since I'd left. Eventually, I met up with my new boss, and he said these fateful words:

"Things have changed since we offered you the job."

What?!

I no longer had total control; HR, Finance, and Customer Services would still report to him. I was responsible for the P&L without authority over it.

It was a recipe for disaster. At that moment, I realised he saw me as a threat, and he wanted to control the situation the owner—not he—had created.
I went back to Holmfield. People welcomed me but were surprised I had come back. I now realised I had made a massive mistake. Again.

The site had deteriorated since I had left. For three months, I tried to pull the site back to where I had left it, but I was constantly blocked by the Operations Director. The staff at Holmfield were nervous because the Ops Director was bringing in his own people to increase his power base. No one wanted to go against him. There was genuine fear.

He was also setting up a factory in the Czech Republic. When he was there, the owners would come to me with their problems. This only annoyed him more. He asked for a budget, so I gave it to him. He said it was not good enough. I reviewed it and sent it to him and the owners. I might as well have signed my own death warrant. The morning I came back from attending my stepdaughter's wedding in Italy, I was met by the Ops Director and the Head of HR—and I was dismissed with three months' wages. They took my phone and PC immediately. The owners were nowhere to be seen. Sacked for the second time. If you don't learn your lessons...

Back in the Trenches

It was the end of September, I was without a job, 57 years old, and didn't have the money to retire. I had to go back to CVs, job interviews, agencies, and coming up with an excuse why my last job had only lasted three months.

In November, I met an HR Director called John Jones from a company called Klockner Pentaplast (kp) at an agency office. I liked him. He was looking for a Black Belt to run technical projects at kp, a plastic food packaging company. The meeting went well. Within two days, he arranged for me to meet Mel Fitton, the Bex Director. He told me to be aware that her bark was worse than her bite. He was bang on. She interviewed me on statistics and CI methodology. It was only when she asked me what Standard Deviation I would accept, and I said "2", that she said, "Correct," and eased off. The job was less money, but John said he would pay me over the Christmas holidays. I accepted. I needed a home. I was battered and bruised. The money was not great, but it was enough.

For the first time ever, I had not seen the factory before accepting a job. On day one, I was taken to my new office, which I shared with five others—the Business Excellence team. It was straight out of Dilbert, the cartoon strip—six cubicles. I sat between a logistics and a lean expert, peeking over my "wall" like Kilroy to the team administrator. Of course, I was the new boy, having to explain about my last job and why I had joined kp. I just told the truth (at least my version of it).

This company was no different to many others—a traditional factory with long-serving employees and the usual stagnant view. "I have worked here for 30 years," which translates as, "I have one year's experience, and it's 30 years old." I had no power to change that. I was there to support large projects—support, not lead. From my time at Bensons and Advanced, where my word was law, or even at Howdens, where my grade gave me some authority, at kp, I was just a Black Belt helping with projects. How the mighty had fallen.

Fair enough. Relax. Let's get on with it. The people were alright, good Yorkshire folk.

Projects on PET flake mountains, European warehouse reductions, stock reductions, packaging initiatives, product wheel, and my favourite, Zero Landfill, followed, plus others. My projects went across both company divisions—FP (food packaging) and PHD (mainly pharmaceutical, labels, and flexibles). I was in the corporate division, in the middle. There were 30 sites, and I communicated with all of them. In the morning, I spoke with Australia, Thailand, and China; in the afternoon, with the UK and Europe; and later, with North and South America. I made friends around the world—some of them have become real friends, not just work friends. I've enjoyed it. I ended up travelling to Germany often, but also to Spain, Italy, the USA, and Canada.

Mel was a great boss—probably one of the best I've had. She would give me a project and then leave me to get on with it. Our fortnightly 1:1s were brief until we talked about her hobby, which was running a hedgehog hospital in her back garden.

For me, my biggest achievement is stopping any waste from going to landfills across all the sites, which the company achieved at the end of 2023. This was directly influenced by my time at Interface and the sustainability vision they had. It was not easy; different countries had different views on sustainability and climate change. In one of the USA sites, they said they loved landfill. It was in West Virginia, the mountain state, where they used landfills to fill in the holes to put golf courses and hospitals on. There, landfill was cheap compared to recycling or waste-to-energy, plus this is a real Republican area where, according to Trump, climate change is not real. When we reduced the waste from 10 tons a day to 10 tons a month, they complained that the food began to smell and sent pictures of black bears wandering around the car park looking for it. At first, I said, didn't they have guns to shoot the bears, or stop eating in the canteen? But eventually, I suggested they double-bag the food waste before throwing it in the compactor. Five thousand miles away, and I was telling them to double-bag food to stop the smell.

Going zero landfill did not save money, but it did not cost as much either once proper recycling procedures were put in place, and it was good for the environment.

Senior management changed regularly, but about six months into my time there, there was a particular large upheaval when the entire Group Senior Management team changed over three months. The owners, a US private equity company, were obviously not happy. Eventually, that included John, which was a shame because I liked him. Our new boss, above Mel, was the COO Alan, who was also a good guy. Three years later, there was another major change, with most of the senior team disappearing. This time, they brought in consultants to make the company more efficient. One site closed, but the corporate functions were hit hard. Of our team, one had already left for the Sales and Operational Team in FP, another had retired, one was transferred to HR, one left, and one was made redundant—this left me.

I was offered the role in FP as the Business Excellence Manager in FP Trays, responsible for the "BEX" improvement in Germany, Italy, the UK, Spain, Poland, Australia, and Belarus, and I gratefully accepted.

Kp has been a good company as I get closer to finishing my career. And it is here that I still am.

CHAPTER SIXTEEN

CONCLUSION OF A LIFE EXAMINED, WHAT HAVE I LEARNED?

So, there you have it. It's not all here, but this is an overview of my life in terms of background, work, and philosophical journey. Only in writing this story have I realised how much my upbringing, time with the CLB, and school affected my future decisions. Talking to people who knew me in those days, who describe me as moody or even angry, explains why I lack patience, have issues with authority, or suffer fools badly today. Or does it?

I wish I had achieved a rational soul as described by Marcus, but I'm not sure I have.

CHARACTERISTICS OF THE RATIONAL SOUL: SELF-PERCEPTION, SELF-EXAMINATION, AND THE POWER TO MAKE OF ITSELF WHATEVER IT WANTS. IT REAPS ITS OWN HARVEST. IT REACHES ITS INTENDED GOAL, NO MATTER WHERE THE LIMIT OF ITS LIFE IS SET. NO MATTER WHICH TASK YOU PICK, IT HAS FULFILLED ITS MISSION AND DONE ITS WORK COMPLETELY. SO THAT IT CAN SAY, 'I HAVE WHAT I CAME FOR.'

MARCUS AURELIUS, MEDITATIONS

Have I fulfilled my mission? What is my mission? To live without fear, to be awake, to be free of opinions and prejudices, to be happy, these seem like good goals. Although I am not there yet, I know what I have to do. Certainly, the School of Philosophy has had a huge impact.

"

CLEANLINESS OF BODY AND MIND. ONE HAS TO LEARN TO CLEAN ONE'S BODY, ONE'S MIND, AND ONE'S HEART, AND FOR THAT, ONE HAS TO FIND A TEACHER.

SHRI SANTANANDA SARASWATI, GOOD COMPANY, 1987, THE STUDY SOCIETY

"

The school gave me a philosophy that made some sort of sense that I could understand. It then challenged me with explaining it to others who challenged me back. The Adwaita philosophy withstood the test. Although I may have issues with the organisation, I do not have issues with the teaching. So, thank you.

There are many other philosophers who also have good things to say, and I have enjoyed reading their thoughts. It's always good to challenge your own opinions, like Descartes.

I have come to the conclusion that I am a hypocrite. I have also decided that so is everyone else and so is this society. I extol meditation but do not do it enough. I drive too fast and sometimes walk past "Big Issue" sellers and beggars on the streets. I have sacked people and been sacked. What am I actually contributing to this world?

Am I asleep?

For yourselves, it is up for you to decide.

But if you are going to be kinder, start with yourself.

So, what can I do about it?

I can find a better way, I hope this book is a start. I can volunteer to help others, and I can challenge the things that are wrong with society. I can wake up.

It has taken thousands of years for this society to evolve. It will take time and effort to change it.

I have definitely made mistakes, but one of the best things about philosophy is that if you are awake, you can do something about it straight away. That does not mean you ignore your errors or that you don't need to deal with the consequences of your bad decisions, but it does mean that you can learn from them and do something positive about your mistakes. Don't be a victim of them.

I try to be good.

Happiness comes from within. Events and people can only make you happy or sad if you let them. Choose to be happy.

"

THERE'S ONLY ONE WAY OF LIFE, AND THAT'S YOUR OWN.

THE LEVELLERS

"

In the book, I describe that your career is your own, but so also is your life. Some are born to advantage, and some are not. Either way, it's up to you how you live your life.

I know that whatever comes my way, be it good or ill, is mine to deal with, and how I deal with it is my responsibility.

> GOD DID NOT INTEND MY HAPPINESS TO REST WITH SOMEONE ELSE.
>
> MARCUS AURELIUS, MEDITATIONS

I am happy, and I aim to continue being so. I have choices. So, my choice is to,

> BE MORE KIND, MY FRIEND; TRY TO BE MORE KIND.
>
> FRANK TURNER

Start with yourself

The adventure continues...

Printed in Great Britain
by Amazon

57881835R00149